The Whisky Roads of Scotland

The Whisky Roads of Scotland

text Derek Cooper   *photographs* Fay Godwin

publisher Jill Norman & Hobhouse Ltd

Jill Norman & Hobhouse Ltd
90 Great Russell Street, London WC1B 3PY

First published, 1982
© text, Derek Cooper, 1982
© photographs, Fay Godwin, 1982

Typeset by Inforum Ltd, Portsmouth
Printed and bound in Hong Kong by
Everbest Printing Co., Ltd.

British Library Cataloguing in Publication Data

Cooper, Derek.
  The whisky roads of Scotland.
  1. Whiskey – Scotland – History
  2. Distilling industries – Scotland
  – History
  I. Title   II. Godwin, Fay
  3384'766352'09411   HD9395.G73S3

ISBN 0-906908-21-3

Designed by Ray Carpenter

I would like to thank the following for assistance and information:
Ewen Mackenzie, Willie Taylor, Brian Spiller, Don Wintle, Stewart McBain, R K Martin,
P D McWilliam, Colin Gibson, Kenneth Maclean, J J Mole, David Grant, Martin
MacDonald, Major Shane Blewitt, Alexander Fenton, Burton Gintell, Mark Lawson,
William Wood, Bill Thomson, Jim Scott, Evan Cattanach, Alan Shiach, Andrew Shand,
Ernest Sharrett, Archie Macpherson, Mike Hewson, Stuart Kershaw.

Derek Cooper, 1981

The photographs are for Judy and Ken Barton, with love and thanks for the idea and
their wonderful help and hospitality.
Special thanks also to Joanna Grimsditch and her welcoming Aberlour Hotel;
to Neil Hendry and Colin Gibson; also to all those generous distilleries who allowed me to
tramp around taking photographs.

Photographic prints made by Helen McQuillan

Fay Godwin, 1981

Frontispiece Old path near Corryhabbie
burn. Beside the burn one can still see
the remains of two old smuggling
bothies.

Contents

Introduction

Anybody who writes about Scotland's most valuable export industry is in luck. For it is rooted not in the grime of towns, but amid scenery of incomparable grandeur. And, to a very great extent, it has stayed there perched on hillsides, snuggled deep beside fast-running burns, set amid farmland and heather moors. There are few managers of distilleries who can't put down their pocket calculator and look out to a view of hills. If you are a countryman at heart, then working in a distillery is the next best thing to being a farmer.

Distilling was as much a part of the farming scene in Moray and Banff as cheese-making is in Leicestershire or cider-making in Devon. The process of malting, mashing, fermenting and double-distilling the barley called for inexhaustible supplies of water. Peat was needed to dry the green malt and fire the copper stills. It was a happy happenstance that the ideal water for making the finest whisky was soft and flowed from the granite mountains. Filtered through beds of heather and mosses compressed into peat, it ran pure and ice-cold. The Highlands, with their high rainfall and moist atmosphere, their foaming brown burns and aromatic peatbanks, turned out to be the perfect place to perform the alchemy that converts grain into *uisge beatha*, the water of life.

There was an additional bonus. The Highlands, in the eighteenth century when the art of distillation came to prominence, were almost gratifyingly inaccessible to the *Sasunnach*, the English, who after the Union of the Parliaments in 1707 began to interfere in the fiscal affairs of the Scots. Their pernicious attempts to introduce a Malt Tax in 1713, similar to the tax levied in England, were followed in 1715 by the rebellious raising of the Jacobite standard in Braemar. As part of the government's plan to quell unrest, a network of military roads was built in the Highlands, but thousands of square miles remained impassable as early travellers from the south found to their discomfort.

The second attempt to overthrow the Hanoverian yoke was as ineffective as the first. When Prince Charles raised his standard at Glenfinnan in 1745, hopes were once again high, but the rout of Culloden put paid to all that. The repressions of 'Butcher' Cumberland and the disarming of the Highlanders damped the fires of war, but if anything gave new impetus to the fires which heated the illicit stills.

Smuggling became a more and more integral part of the peasant economy and the 'whisky' roads that led from remote glens to the towns grew busier by the year. It would not be an exaggeration to say that almost any overgrown paths you encounter in the hills today would at one time have been trodden by smugglers either bringing barley or malt to their whisky bothies or taking their kegs by pony to customers in Inverness, Elgin, Aberdeen, Perth and Dundee. Much of the whisky found its way south to Edinburgh, Stirling and Glasgow and the whisky roads became as well-mapped as the older drove roads through the glens to the trysts of Crieff and Falkirk.

The tracks up to the summer shielings became whisky roads too, for an upland pasture far from the prying eyes of the revenue men was a fine and private place in which to make whisky. Plenty of peat and water, plenty enough of time. Today when your eye falls on a modern-looking distillery with its asbestos roof and dark grains plant, don't be deceived. It may have been renovated and rebuilt over the years, but more than likely it will be there because two centuries ago some enter-prising freebooter decided to do his own thing on that very spot. The lone shieling, the remote farmhouse by the burn, the bothy on the seashore now bear names respected wherever fine malt whisky is prized. *Glenlivet, Balmenach, Cardow, Macallan, Lochnagar, Highland Park, Glenturret, Ardbeg, Dailuaine, Lagavulin, Ord* . . . all rose on the site of unlicensed stills. It was a transition which took a lot of excitement out of life. After the passing of the 1823 Act to Eliminate Illicit Distilling there were fewer broken heads on the whisky roads, but the smuggling continued fitfully, for the sporting instinct dies hard. There are some who believe that it still survives.

The three great centres of distilling in Victorian times were in the Mull of Kintyre, centred on Campbeltown (a hundred years ago there were 21 distilleries, today there are only two), in Islay (nine a hundred years ago and eight today) and that golden triangle in the north-east corner of Scotland centred on Elgin, Rothes, Keith and Dufftown. It is this last region on which we have concentrated.

As to the old whisky roads themselves, they are mere tracks many of which you'll need an Ordnance Survey map to find and stout boots to walk. The whisky roads of today have unromantic names like B9009, B9014 and A95; they are cluttered in the summer with coaches and unlovely mobile homes, but in the winter juggernauts laden with barley and butts of whisky have it mostly to themselves. Happily the landscape remains almost unchanged; taking to the hills is to walk back a century and more. No whisky-laden pack-horses on Cairn o'Mount, Glen Clova, the Ladder or the Fungle these days, no peat-fires in the heather. But once upon a time . . .

Opposite   Site of illicit still, Corryhabbie burn. In these parts the eighteenth-century pioneer of illicit distilling was Robbie Macpherson of Glenrinnes. He migrated to Upper Folds, Corryhabbie and set up home with his wife Margaret one summer in what was little more than a tinker's tent. Before winter came on he had constructed a more impermeable dwelling out of heather and turf divots. Then he began working a derelict croft nearby and in his spare time took up whisky-making. After the passing of the Wash Act in 1784 he began to be plagued by visits from the gaugers. Tired of the frequent infringements of his freedom he moved his apparatus up to a secluded and, he hoped, inaccessible part of the burn.

Macpherson didn't sell his spirit straight from the still but gave it time to mature in oak ankers hidden in caches dug in the hillside. Robbie and the other Glenrinnes smugglers took their *uisge* by horse and cart in heavily manned convoys to sea ports like Buckie, the whisky concealed among bales of wool, sacks of barley and innocent kegs of butter. Sympathisers in Dufftown alerted the Corryhabbie smugglers to any alarming movements from the Excisemen by lighting warning beacons on the Conval hill and the clandestine distillers had a long and secure run for their money.

1 This Traffic Operates Like a Secret Poison

As far as I know the Scots are the only race in the world to have an internationally renowned drink named after them and that is surprising because 'Scotch' was only invented in the middle of the nineteenth century.

The art of distilling strong waters from barley had been practised in Scotland from the fifteenth century onwards, maybe even earlier, but it is unlikely that these medieval distillations bore much relation to whisky as we know it today. Herbs and spices were added frequently for medicinal purposes but more practically to make the ardent spirit more palatable. *Usquebaugh* as it was known in Ireland or *uisge beatha*, to give it its Gaelic translation, was almost invariably improved with spices and even fruit. In his dictionary published in 1755 before he had actually set foot in Scotland, Dr. Johnson defined whisky as 'a compound distilled spirit being drawn on aromaticks'.

It was the kind of all-purpose spirit which could be drunk with sugar and hot water as a toddy or used as a base for cordials and punches flavoured with cinnamon and cloves. As the techniques of fermentation and distillation became more refined *uisge* became acceptable enough to be drunk on its own and the dram was born. But for much of the eighteenth century whisky was less in evidence than rum, brandy and claret which was rowed ashore on some desolate beach and taken by pack-horse to the thirsty interior. The most widely consumed beverage was beer; there never was in Gaelic a word for whisky-house. The common name for an inn was *Tigh-Leanne*, ale-house. The poor drank strong frothing ale from the cask in wooden cups; the lairds drank wines and brandy smuggled in from the Low Countries and France.

In the whole of Boswell's *Journal* describing his epic journey with Samuel Johnson to the Hebrides in 1773, there are only a few brief references to whisky. At Dunvegan Castle the travellers were entertained like princes by Lady Macleod who laid venison pasty and roast beef before them for dinner. 'She has,' noted Boswell, 'at the same time the greatest economy. She is butler herself, even of the porter. We had porter from the cask, as in London; claret, port, sherry and punch. The claret we soon quitted. Macleod and Talisker and I drank port. The rest of the men drank punch.'

Farm land near Glen Buchat.

On the Ladder near Glen Buchat. Bounded on the north by the Cabrach and on the south by Strathdon, Glen Buchat had a population of 500 in the early nineteenth century. On the lower ground the light loamy soil and an abundance of limestone for fertilising the land made it a rich farming centre. Depopulated now by the drift to the towns it is prowled by combine harvesters and the occasional passing car.

At Raasay House a few weeks earlier, where they had been entertained by Macleod of Raasay, they were given a substantial dinner and a variety of wines. The dram or *sgailc* they were offered on arrival was brandy not whisky, and with the mutton chops and tarts there was porter, claret, mountain, punch, coffee and tea.

Thirty-nine years earlier, Prince Charles Edward Stuart, on the run from Cumberland's troops after the shambles of Culloden, took not whisky but a bottle of brandy with him from Raasay on his flight to Morar. In earlier times the Norsemen who dominated the islands of the north and west drank ale and mead, not spirits; Macbeth called for wine not whisky to drown his guilt after Duncan's murder. And the epic carouses of eighteenth-century Scotland came from hogsheads of smuggled claret. When Lord Lovat entertained two dozen guests at Beaufort Castle in 1739, he ordered 'John Forbes to send in horses for all Lachlan Macintosh's wine and for six dozen of the Spanish wine'.

There is ample evidence that heavy and prolonged drinking bouts relieved the tedium of country life. A hogshead of claret stood in many a nobleman's hall and a contemporary writer claimed that 'a landlord was considered inhospitable who permitted any of his guests to retire without their requiring the assistance of his servants. Those who tarried for the night found in the bedrooms a copious supply of ale, wine and brandy to allay the thirst super-induced by their previous potations.' And even when you staggered from your bed to effect a befuddled departure, your strength of purpose was further delayed by a bumper at the door, the traditional *deoch-an-doruis* which could be the prelude to another round of festivities.

No rituals were more drink-sodden than those which attended an interment, and the more distinguished the corpse the more monumental the carousing. When The Chisholm died in 1817, his body lay in state for several days at an inn in Inverness where wines and refreshments were laid out for all visitors. 'A banquet', the county history records, 'was held in a granary close to Beauly Priory where he was buried. Those of "gentle kindred" occupied the upper room while the commons caroused in the lower storey. Claret, it is said "ran like ditch-water" and the old women of the village brought pails to carry off the superfluous whisky and are said to have kept public-houses for six months afterwards on the relics of the feast.'

By that time, whisky had become the national tipple and Robert Burns, the country's first national poet, had emerged as its champion and chronicler. It was he who first identified the nation with John Barleycorn and focused contempt on those who were framing the excise laws in London. In 'The Author's Cry and Prayer', he asked:

Is there, that bears the name of Scot
But feels his heart's bluid rising hot,

To see his poor auld mither's pot
Thus dung in staves,
And plundered o' her hindmost groat
By gallows knaves?

All right-thinking readers, said Burns, should rally to the cause of getting 'auld Scotland' her kettle back and if persuasion didn't work, force would follow:

An' Lord, if ance they pit her till't
Her tartan petticoat she'll kilt,
An' durk an' pistol at her belt,
She'll tak the streets
An' rin her whittle to the hilt
I' th' first she meet.

An illicit still on display at *Glenfarclas* reception centre. Compared with the six big stills of *Glenfarclas* this is a small trespass indeed against the State. Notice that the main body of the still itself had no head elevation and unpleasant impurities like fusel oil and acids would all pass into the cooling worm along with the vapourised alcohol. Barnard describes how such a still operated in a purpose built bothy at Cromdale: 'It possesses an underground spring, wherein the little coil or worm which condenses the precious spirit was laid, and at a lower level it dipped into a receiver made out of an earthen jar some two feet high with a wooden lid thereon. The little copper still stood on a furnace made with the loose stones that had fallen from the rock behind, and the mash tun had originally been a wash tub. The place was totally dark and no light was ever permitted except that which came from the furnace fire'.

For one so dedicated to freedom – 'whisky and freedom gang thegither' – and the dignity of man, his acceptance of a post in the Excise in 1791 is as shocking as a betrayal. Not long before, Dr Johnson had defined 'Excise' as 'a hateful tax levied upon commodities, and judged not by the common judges of property, but by wretches hired by those to whom Excise is paid'. By the time Burns joined the enemy, home-made whisky had begun to replace brandy, rum and gin in the festive punch bowl. The gentry still favoured imported wine and spirits, but the ordinary people were gradually moving from ale to whisky.

By the second decade of the nineteenth century, when illicit distilling reached its peak, whisky-drinking had become inseparably linked with both work and play. Writing of events in 1812, Elizabeth Grant of Rothiemurchus recalled that 'in the pantry a bottle of whisky was the allowance per day, with bread and cheese in any required quantity. The very poorest cottages could offer whisky; all the men engaged in the wood manufacture drank it in goblets three times a day'.

A year later she visited the men who were cutting down the great Rothiemurchus pine forest and floating the logs down the Spey to the coast. 'The men probably had their private dram before beginning the day . . . a lad with a small cask – a quarter anker – on his back, and a horn cup in his hand that held a gill, appeared three times a day amongst them. They all took their "morning" raw, undiluted and without accompaniment, so they did the gill at parting when the day was done; but the noontide dram was part of a meal. Sometimes a floater's wife or bairn would come up with a message; such messenger was always offered whisky. Aunt Mary had a story that one day a woman with a child in her arms, and another bit thing at her knee, came up among them; the horn cup was duly handed to her, she took a "gey guid drap" herself, and then gave a little to each of the babies. "My goodness, child," said my mother to the wee thing that was trotting by the mother's side, "doesn't it *bite* you?" "Ay, but I like the bite", replied the creature.'

This would have been smuggler's whisky, most likely overproof, probably rough and unmatured, certainly untaxed. As illicit distilling increased, whisky became the currency of the country. Eighteenth-century travellers in Scotland frequently found that coinage was conspicuously absent and most local transactions were conducted in terms of barter and not species. Even a land-owner might be permanently short of coin, his rents being paid in yarn, poultry, salmon, pigs, sheep, barley, oats, pease and straw or whatever the ground produced. In the richer lands of Morayshire and Aberdeen, the ground produced both bere and barley and it was the custom for the surplus to be converted into whisky. If you left barley in the girnal or granary it could very often be spoiled by damp or eaten by rats, but distilled it immediately became portable, potable and an acceptable currency of the realm.

There was a natural bonus in distilling. A contemporary account in 1813 explained that 'the grain consumed in distillation is not wholly lost in human food. It has been ascertained that as much milk, beef, pork, or other animal food can be raised from the draff and dreg, after the spirit is extracted, as could have been produced upon the land on which the barley grew, had it been sown with grass and thrown into pasture.' Indeed the cattle feed made available by winter distilling prevented many a beast from being prematurely slaughtered or sent to market at the end of summer.

Rents were paid in whisky and many landlords provided barley for those tenants who lived on land too barren to grow grain. The barley, when malted and mashed and distilled, was handed back for consumption by the laird or over to smugglers who would spirit it stealthily by night to the nearest town.

Smuggling was endemic in those days. It took two forms. The oldest tradition was the importation of contraband cargoes from the Continent. In the Shetland and Orkney isles, smuggled casks were frequently deposited in churches for safekeeping and there were few ministers who asked questions when an anker of brandy was left at the manse door. So respectable a part of trading life was the running of dutiable goods into the fishing ports of Scotland that Coutts, the merchants and bankers of Edinburgh, had a colleague in Rotterdam whose principal activity lay in providing goods for the smugglers who sailed between Holland and the ports of north-east Scotland.

Those who dealt in contraband stood high in public esteem. Not only were they keeping prices down they were also, by evading excise duty, cocking a snook at 'our auld enemies of England'. Many smugglers, as Professor Walker, a nineteenth-century Scottish historian, wrote, 'constituted a sort of recognised corporation, claiming a rank second to that

A re-creation at *Glenfarclas* of what a smuggling bothy might have looked like. Bothies were often so skilfully camouflaged that they took a lot of finding; very often it was only the tell-tale escape of smoke that would betray the distiller to the excisemen.

Strenuous efforts were made to funnel the smoke to where it might be mistaken for the product of an innocent fire. Some smugglers built long flues from their bothies so that the smoke would mingle with the smoke from the hearth in a nearby house. Steve Sillett in *Illicit Scotch* tells of a smuggler at the Falls of Orrin who built his chimney in such a way that the smoke blended perfectly with the spray from the waterfall. Tradition has it that the clock tower in the centre of Dufftown was once used as an illicit distillery, the smoke issuing from a narrow chimney resembling a lightning conductor.

Fettercairn set amid corn fields; a reminder that distilling sprang direct from the cycle of the farming year. Lying close to the village the distillery was built above the river North Esk; it takes its water from the summit of the nearby Grampians which were once seething with smugglers. The distillery itself was originally established two miles higher up on the slopes of Cairn o' Mount, but when a larger distillery was built in 1824 the old works were abandoned. The whisky is sold under the name of Old Fettercairn. I'm told, although I cannot find any written authority for it, that the distillery once stood on the Highland Line which ran through Kirriemuir, Edzell, Fettercairn and Cairn o' Mount. It was moved to the fiscally favourable side of the village to take advantage of the lower rates of duty. True or not I can't establish. But here's a vivid *Fettercairn* memory given me by the Rev. Harry Ricketts who was brought up in the village: 'In my lifetime the old casks, some of which had been used for maturing spirit for fifty years and more, would be given to the workers as a perk. They would pour in a couple of gallons of boiling water and then roll them up and down Whisky Raw, as the row where the distillery stood was known. After the hot water and steam had circulated round and round the cask any whisky in the wood would have been extracted and they'd wind up with a couple of very good gallons for themselves. It was known as "grogging the cask" but the practice was made illegal just before the Great War'.

of the landowners, and bearing themselves as the *petite noblesse* of the community. In church they occupied as a body the front pew of the gallery which was spoken of as the "smugglers loft" and this not sneeringly but with a feeling of respect. The illegality of their employment was forgotten or disregarded in a neighbourhood where persons of all ranks were openly and unscrupulously their customers . . . The smugglers dwelt in excellent houses, wore fine clothes, rode showy horses and exercised a cordial hospitality.'

Two stories illustrate the ambivalence of high and low to breaking both the law of the land and the law of God. The first was told by Alfred Barnard about an old wifie who lived near the old *Hazelburn* distillery in Campbeltown. She was hauled before the Sheriff on a smuggling charge which was swiftly proven.

'I daresay, my poor woman, it is not often you have been guilty of this fault,' said the Sheriff before pronouncing sentence.

'Deed no, Sheriff. I haena made a drap since youn wee keg I sent to yersel.'

And then there was the minister who, meeting a parishioner noted for the excellence of his illicit whisky, pointed out the wickedness of his ways. He received an indignant reply:

'I alloo nae swearin' at the still and everything's dune dacently and in order; I canna see ony harm in't!'

There was not one soul in their right mind who saw any harm in it. In remote places, whole communities were engaged either in making whisky or smuggling it to the point of sale. On the Solway Firth there was neither trade nor industry and when questioned about their livelihood the answer was invariably: 'We smuggle a little.' Honest fishermen abandoned their nets in favour of brandy-running and working an illicit still was regarded as a worthier occupation than working the land.

One of the most infamous smuggling villages on the east coast was Collieston, fifteen miles north of Aberdeen. Its sandy cove, now a weekend resort for Aberdonians, at one time housed the notorious Philip Kennedy who was fatally injured by an exciseman during a particularly violent clash. So prevalent was smuggling in the area that it attracted the most ambitious exciseman of all, the ill-fated Malcolm Gillespie.* When he was appointed to the Aberdeen Collection in the early years of the nineteenth century, he focused his attention on Collieston where more than a thousand ankers of contraband spirits were being landed every month. So successful was Gillespie in his battles with the smugglers, that they were forced to abandon Collieston and remove their activities to Skateraw and Braidon bays. But Gillespie pursued them there and beyond to Stonehaven where, in zealous

---

* For a fuller account of the intrepid Gillespie see pages 41–44

Remains of an old still site at Corryhabbie. Many such bothies were as comfortable as a sheiling with makeshift beds, a larder for food and of course plenty of home-made liquid cheer.

Opposite Mount Keen and Glen Tanar. The first stretch of the glen is well wooded and if you take the South Deeside road from Aboyne you can leave your car at Braeloine car park where there is an excellent visitor centre and ecological exhibition. In the old days the people lived by trafficking in timber, mainly fir trees; hence the name 'Fir Mounth', the pass over the Grampians taken by the invading armies of Edward I. Today there are raw and deplorable Land Rover tracks scarring the hills. Ill-made and unmetalled they contribute grievously to erosion and are an affront to the eye.

co-operation with the officers of the revenue cutters, he made life miserable for large numbers of people. During his time at Collieston and Stonehaven, he seized 14,000 gallons of foreign spirits, 33 horses and their carts and destroyed 1,800 gallons of contraband brandy. He and his men also discovered 37 illicit stills and confiscated a thousand gallons of whisky; all this in one small corner of Aberdeen. But it was a trade rife all over the Highlands and one which grew over the years.

It is estimated that in 1708 only 51,000 gallons of whisky were distilled in Scotland, but seventy years later 300,000 gallons were crossing the border every year without paying a penny excise. Customs officers were opposed by all right-thinking men and women and it frequently required the support of a detachment of troops to outwit a determined bunch of smugglers.

There were many incentives to manufacture whisky illicitly, particularly in the Highlands. Here amid the remote straths and glens there was no industry and no gainful employment apart from such agricultural pursuits as the hostile climate and a frequently barren land would allow. 'Let the Highlanders', wrote Colonel David Stewart in 1822, 'remain a pastoral and agricultural people, the superabundant population filling our military ranks with good recruits, sending out an annual supply of labourers to the low country when required and colonizing our distant possessions with a loyal and well-principled race.' To which, had they been able to read *Sketches of the Character, Manners and Present State of the Highlanders of Scotland*, those same Highlanders might well have stuck two prominent fingers up in the air and returned to their stills. And in a way they had a great deal of right on their side. In 1814, a fatuous Act of Parliament decreed that north of a line running along the southern base of the Grampians all distillation was prohibited in stills holding less than 500 gallons of wash.

A further interdict on selling Highland spirit south of the Highland line, a prohibition introduced to protect the Lowland distillers, meant in effect that the legal distilling of whisky in the Highlands became impossible. As Colonel Stewart correctly wrote, 'a still of this magnitude would consume more than the disposable grain in the most extensive country within this newly drawn boundary; nor could fuel be obtained for such an establishment without an expense that the commodity could not possibly bear [and] the market which alone could have supported the manufacture was entirely cut off.'

The Act meant in practice that small farmers unable to afford the expense of sending their surplus grain to the Lowland distillers, where its frequently inferior quality commanded only minimal prices, were unable to pay their rents. There was no alternative for them but to resort to illicit distillation of their barley, the only negotiable asset of the farming year.

The laws and regulations governing distillation were difficult to

Packhorse bridge at Aberlour over the Lour burn. Robert Duff, a local mason, was given £5 in 1729 to repair the bridge which may well date from the seventeenth century.

understand and unsuited to the rural Highland economy, frequently poised after a poor harvest on the edge of famine. As the Rev. David Dunoon of Killearnan in Ross-shire wrote in 1796, 'distilling is almost the only method of converting our victual into cash for the payment of rents and servants; and what may in fact be called our staple commodity.' John Stein, a Lowland distiller, giving evidence to the government Committee on Distilleries in 1798, revealed that by then distilling had spread over the whole countryside and to every island from the Orkneys to Jura. 'There are many who practise this art who are ignorant of every other, and there are distillers who boast that they make the best possible whiskey, who cannot read or write and who carry on the manufacture in parts of the country where the use of the plough is unknown and the face of the Exciseman is never seen.'

When you could convert a shilling's worth of malt into four shillings' worth of whisky without too much effort, it is not surprising that everyone with access to bere or barley was an amateur alchemist. It is not too far-fetched to make the parallel between home wine-making in Britain today and domestic distilling in eighteenth-century Scotland. Everyone with time on their hands was having a go. On many farms, the task of making whisky was delegated to maidservants – in much the same way that dandelion and parsnip wine-making in England would have been a woman's responsibility not a man's.

Just as today you can buy your Campden tablets and fermentation lock in Boots, so in the eighteenth century any smith would run you up a still. 'So general was smuggling at Inverness,' it was observed, 'there were two or three master coppersmiths who had a sign above their shops of a whisky still, indicating their employment.'

A fascinating insight into the craft of still-making is revealed in the Still Books of Robert Armour,* who established himself as a plumber and coppersmith in Campbeltown in 1811. The plumber's shop was the front for a highly efficient manufactory of four parts, the vessel itself into which the fermented wash was poured, the head, the arm and the worm. A ten-gallon still could be had for about £5. Armour also made tin stills which were much cheaper, but corroded comparatively quickly. Most stills were owned by a consortium varying in numbers from three to seven. They would share the initial cost of the apparatus and be responsible for the distilling operation and the moving of the still from place to place if detection was imminent. The stills were paid for sometimes in cash, sometimes in whisky, peat, meal, potatoes, cheese and butter. Ten gallons of whisky could have bought a still, so that initial outlay was well within the reach of even the poorest.

* I am indebted to 'A Maker of Illicit Stills', an article in *Scottish Studies* (Volume 14: 1970) by I. A. Glen who was given access to the Still Books of Robert Armour, Campbeltown, then in the possession of R. R. Armour of Edinburgh.

2 An Infamous and Demoralizing Practice

Various travellers in the Western Isles at the turn of the century noted the irresistible temptation which distillation presented to the poor and they noted too that grain which should have gone into feeding people went instead for distillation. 'This distillation', wrote John Leyden in 1803, 'had a most ruinous effect in increasing the scarcity of grain last year, particularly in Isla and Tiree where the people subsisted chiefly on fish and potatoes.'

When in 1782 the harvest failed in the Mull of Kintyre, the Commissioners of Supply ordered all the illicit stills in Argyll to be confiscated, hoping in that way to make more grain available for feeding the poor. The shortage of corn which resulted from the Napoleonic wars brought about a further prohibition of whisky-making from 1795 to 1797, but there is no evidence that anyone took the slightest notice.

What such whisky tasted like will now never be known, but for a long period it was regarded as greatly superior to the whisky produced by the licensed distillers of the Lowlands. To cut the high costs imposed by the tax on malt, the legal distillers used a high proportion of unmalted grain; often the malted barley content of their mash was as low as twenty per cent. The freeland distillers, untroubled by duty, made their whisky entirely from malted grain.

On the other hand, a lot of illicit whisky was made not from barley but bere. I have only tasted bere once in my life and that was in Orkney, where small quantities are still grown, principally I imagine as a curiosity. Bere or *hordeum sativum vulgare*, to give it its botanic name, was popular in the Hebrides and the far north because it did better than barley on thin soil and ripened more easily in latitudes where the growing season was short. In the early years of the nineteenth century, half the grain grown in islands like Tiree, Mull and Islay was bere, and indeed a few legal distilleries, *Highland Park* notable amongst them, continued to use bere in preference to barley until the end of the last century. Bere was also widely in use in Campbeltown until the 1860s. Bere contained less sugars than barley and it therefore yielded less alcohol; for that reason it paid a smaller duty – ninepence a bushel compared with two shillings for barley in the 1820s.

The legally made whisky must have been poor stuff indeed if the contraband was preferred. In the first place, although all the grain used was malted, the method of production was often hit and miss. Distilling was always attended with the risk of discovery and the techniques were often of necessity primitive: no thermometers, no elaborate technical safeguards, no custom-built utensils. Frequently the grain would be steeped in a muddy pool and then spread out on the floor of a hut or in a cave to germinate. In a modern maltings the temperature is carefully controlled so that the germination of the grain can occur in optimum conditions. Making whisky on a hillside was, to say the least, pragmatic.

John Macculloch, the traveller and geologist who journeyed widely in the Hebrides in the early years of the nineteenth century, was afforded many ringside glimpses of the illicit distiller going about his alfresco pursuits. In the decade or so before government changed its policies and made legal distilling more profitable than illegal, it was almost impossible for a voyager in the remoter parts of the Highlands and Islands not to stumble upon smugglers either actually making the stuff or stealthily conveying it to the point of sale. 'The malting', wrote Macculloch, 'is generally carried on by a distinct class, by the dealers in grain themselves; and the wash is manufactured in a rude hut in some retired or concealed spot poorly provided with a few casks and tubs. The remainder of the apparatus consists of two or three casks to receive the spirit and of a still, generally of eighteen gallons in capacity and with a very short worm and tub; the great command of water rendering a long one unnecessary. Sometimes a hut is erected to protect the still from the weather; but it is frequently set up in the open air, under some bank or rock which permits a stream of water to be easily introduced into the tub.'

Macculloch has left a vivid portrait of a minor skirmish on the island of Lismore in Loch Linnhe which probably took place at about the time of the more memorable Battle of Waterloo. On his jaunts round the islands, Macculloch was able to make use of the facilities provided by the revenue men and he frequently sailed with them, he with his scholarly eye alert for curious formations of strata, they with their predatory eyes straining for a tell-tale wisp of peat smoke. And then on the morning in question, an alert member of the crew spotted just such an illicit plume rising in the still summer air. The cutter altered course, crammed on sail and made for the shore. 'Beneath a rock, close by the edge of the water was burning a bright and clear fire near which sat an old man and a young girl with two or three casks scattered about. An iron crook suspended on some rude poles supported a still and the worm passed into a tall cask into which fell a small stream from the summit of the rock behind. Two or three sturdy fellows were lounging about; while the alchemist sat over the fire, in the attitude of Geber or Paracelsus waiting for the moment of projection.'

Opposite Corgarff castle, perched on the skyline like a toy, was built in 1537. In 1571 when the Gordons and Forbeses were feuding a Captain Ker immolated Margaret Campbell, wife of John Forbes of Towie within its grim walls. All her family and retainers – twenty seven men, women and children – perished in the murderous attack which was celebrated in the ballad 'Edom o' Gordon'.

The keep was restored by the Earl of Mar and was burned once again by the Jacobites in 1689. During the rebellion of 1745 it was used as an arsenal. When 400 Hanoverian troops reached it in February 1746 it had been abandoned by the rebels 'but so lately that the fire was burning and no living creature in the house but a poor cat sitting by the fire'. It was converted into a barracks during the savage reprisals which followed Bonnie Prince Charlie's final defeat at Culloden.

A captain, a subaltern and 56 men remained at the castle until 1831 to assist the gaugers in their attempts to stamp out illicit distillation and smuggling in Glenavon and the Ladder Hills. By then the original tower had been extended and a star-shaped curtain wall had been constructed, pierced for muskets like the ramparts at Braemar castle. Corgarff stands 1,416 feet above sea level on the old military road to Braemar, a lone outpost in wild ountry.

Macculloch espied a rude shed built under the shelter of another rock which seemed to contain a few tubs and casks: 'nor could anything be more picturesque than this primitive laboratory or more romantic than the whole scene.' But Macculloch had only a split second to take the tableau in. 'Before the boat was well in sight, an universal scream was set up; away ran the girl to some cottages which were perched on the cliff and down came men, women and children, hallooing, scolding, swearing and squalling, in all the unappreciable intonations of a Gaelic gamut; the still-head was whipt up by a sturdy virago, the malt was thrown out, the wash emptied.' The excisemen leapt ashore and the still was captured. Owing to Macculloch's entreaties, the rest of the plunder was returned to the islanders.

It was much easier for the revenue men to patrol the islands than the mainland wilderness. The sea was a road open to them all the year round except during the season of the ferocious winter gales. But in the Highlands, roads were completely absent and contraband had to be hauled over tracks which were often more fit for feral goats than pack-horses and ponies.

In the aftermath of the 1715 Jacobite rebellion and the invasion of Wester Ross by a Spanish army*, George I despatched General Wade north to see what he could do to prevent a recurrence of these wild insurrections. Between 1723 and 1740, Wade, as Commander-in-Chief of North Britain, built 250 miles of military roads and forty bridges. It was an ambitious project, but it did no more than provide a link between the garrisons at strategically important centres like Fort George near Inverness, Fort Augustus at the western end of Loch Ness, and Fort William.

By the end of the eighteenth century, the remoter sections of Wade's roads had crumbled away and were little more than rough tracks. A vivid picture of travelling the really bad stretches has been left behind in a diary kept by John Stanhope, who travelled to Skye in the year 1806. Deep in the Highlands, he and his companion Archibald Macdonald, brother of the eighteenth Chief of Sleat, stayed the night at the Dalwhinnie inn which had originally been built by Wade as his personal residence. The inn was so overcrowded, the consumption of *uisge* on so great a scale, that its smell 'pervaded every corner of the house so powerfully that any teetotaller would have committed a breach of his oath by merely inhaling the air'.

The following day they set off to scale Wade's road to Fort Augustus which crossed the 2,500-foot Corrieyairack Mountain. 'The road was execrable and we picked our way with difficulty. In a short time we

Invercauld bridge, Braemar. To the east of Braemar the 'bright snow-fed Dee' which flows from the summit of Braeriach 85 miles to the North Sea at Aberdeen is crossed by two bridges. This four-arched one was built in 1753 to carry the military road from Blairgowrie on its route north by Glen Gairn to Corgarff and thence on to Fort George at Inverness.

* In April 1719, a group of Spaniards landed from frigates in Loch Duich and quartered themselves at Donan castle in support of the Jacobite cause. It took several weeks to muster an army in Inverness which marched to Glen Shiel and routed the Jacobites and their Spanish mercenaries on June 11.

found ourselves at the foot of the long-dreaded Corryarrick. It was six miles to the top of it and three down the other side. With all the spirit that our wet and frozen limbs permitted we began to ascend. The road was a zigzag, the surface covered with large, loose stones and every now and then it degenerated into steps cut through a rock. Thus we staggered on, in the middle of a dreadful rain, abetted by a most violent wind, so that we were wet to the skin and frozen to numbness by the sharpness of the gale.' After Fort Augustus, the way to the western seaboard was even more daunting. 'There had once, I believe, been a road . . . made by General Wade. It was composed of rocks and loose stones, and variegated with rivers and bogs which the great quantity of rain that had fallen rendered very deep and dangerous.'

It was this collapsing network that Thomas Telford, the genius of the age, inherited at the beginning of the last century when he began his remarkable Scottish road-building programme. Under his direct supervision, 730 miles of road and a thousand bridges were built, a labour that opened up the Highlands. Invited in 1803 to submit proposals to improve matters, Telford reported that 'previous to the year 1742 the roads were merely the tracks of black cattle and horses intersected by numerous rapid streams which being frequently swollen into torrents by heavy rains rendered them dangerous and impassable.'

Telford was an almost universal provider, designing churches and piers with equal enthusiasm. Readers following the whisky trail should note near Aberlour one of his most elegant achievements, Craigellachie Bridge. Foremost among the fine cast-iron bridges of Britain and the first of any size to be built in Scotland, it has a single 150-foot-long span with four ribs arching airily above the Spey. Its castellated terminals hold a plate bearing the legend 'cast at Plas Kynaston Ruabon Denbighshire 1814'.

But even Telford couldn't do anything about the weather. We're not much better off today. There are snow ploughs to keep the main roads open, but in the winter life in the wilder glens comes almost to a standstill. The small community who live in and around Cock Bridge, 1,350 feet above sea level, is used to being completely marooned in the winter. When I first went there, although the Hydro Board's cables swung by overhead, the few scattered houses remained unconnected to the national grid. Each family relied on its 'jennie' and if the generator went then it was back to paraffin lamps and candles.

Cock Bridge lies on the boundary between what used to be Aberdeenshire and Banffshire. The road, the second highest in Scotland, rises to more than 2,100 feet before it descends to Tomintoul which claims, however reluctantly, to be the highest village in Scotland. It wasn't built until twenty years after the military road was driven from Corgarff to Abernethy on the Spey. This is barren country where grim

Bridge at Strathdon.

Landscape near Tomintoul.

The Beatshach lying between the Spey valley and Glen Rinnes, four miles south of Aberlour.

Landscape, Glen Rinnes. The countryside of what was once known as Upper Banffshire is remote and although well-farmed is still unspoilt.

tales are told of travellers buried in snowdrifts, their bodies only uncovered in the thaw of the following spring.

'The crops', observed an early agricultural reporter of this high and mountainous region, 'are for the most part damaged by rains, which about October often set in for weeks together and are frequently succeeded without any interval of good weather by frosts and deep falls of snow which often suspend the operations of husbandry for many of the winter months.' A terrain sufficient to daunt the most indomitable, the most persevering; one in which you needed strong spirits to keep your spirits up. No wonder so many turned to the still for cheap and illicit comfort.

It has been said and repeated over the years that at one time there were 200 stills in the Glenlivet area alone. In the summer of 1980 I was talking to an old man who lived in Chapeltown of Glenlivet. He too assured me that there had been 200. The figure worries me. If, as seems to be the case, five or more men would be co-operating in the running of a still, then that would mean a minimum of a thousand men, and it is highly unlikely that the glen could ever have supported a thousand men and their families. Even if each still was operated by one family, that would mean 200 families in Glenlivet and there are today no traces of such a desperate over-population. And yet the figure runs like a rune through all the literature on the subject. Alfred Barnard, when he visited Glenlivet in the 1880s, was told that 'formerly smuggling houses were scattered on every rill, all over the mountain glens and at that time the smugglers used to lash the kegs of spirit on their backs and take them all the way to Aberdeen and Perth for disposal.'

Steve Sillett, in his entertaining *Illicit Scotch*, gives an even giddier figure, estimating that in Glenlivet, Glenrinnes and Cabrach there were 400 stills at work. But perhaps I'm wrong, maybe such high estimates are indeed accurate. A minister of Strathdon, which in 1801 had a population of 1,354, estimated that in the early part of the nineteenth century smuggling was endemic. A large part of the parish, much of it wild upland, was, he said, before the Act of 1823 which rendered legal distillation more profitable, a stronghold of smuggling. 'The inhabitants of Corgarff, the glens and not a few in the lower part of the parish were professed smugglers. The revenue officers were set at defiance. To be engaged in illicit distillation, and to defraud the excise, was neither looked on as a crime, nor considered as a disgrace. As may be supposed, such a system of things proved most pernicious, productive of the grossest demoralization, irreligion, and sin, destructive of every habit of regular industry.'

But then a happy change took place. 'By the vigorous measures adopted by the Government, effectively seconded by the proprietors, this moral pest was struck at the very root and speedily became utterly extinct. The lawless life of the smuggling "bothie" was wholly abandoned and the honest labours of agriculture substituted. It is a subject of just congratulation to contemplate the industrious spirit, the healthy tone of moral feeling and the fixed religious principle that are gradually, under the blessing of God, acquiring more and more strength over their minds.'

There is no doubt that just as the population of the Hebrides reached its peak at the time of the highest demand for kelp and fell sharply when the seaweed lost its commercial value, so the population of the smuggling glens began to decline as the legal distilleries took over from the small illicit stills. In Strathdon, for instance, there were 1,570 people in 1827; by 1831 fewer than 1,490. The cause of the growth and decline in population was undoubtedly the rise and fall of illicit distillation.

'While this infamous and demoralizing practice prevailed,' one reads in the *Statistical Account of Aberdeenshire* of 1843, 'population increased through the facilities by which families were maintained among the hills and valleys on its profits. But no sooner was this system put down, than the effect appeared on population. Fewer marriages than formerly now take place, and a considerable number of families, formerly supported by illicit distillation, have been obliged to remove to towns and other parishes: a good many families also, have emigrated to America.'

Walk these glens today and, except at holiday time when the ramblers come out from the towns, you'll have the place almost entirely to yourself. But a century and a half ago it presented a scene of covert alchemy by day and clandestine movement by night. Had you taken the whisky trail up the Spey valley, round the slopes of Ben Rinnes, through the Howe of the Mearns, over the Ladder Hills, down the Dullan Water and up the Lecht to Glenlivet a hundred years ago, you would have found dozens of men who, as youngsters, would have warmed their hands on an illicit still. Folk heroes like James Smith were still working their illicit stills alongside the legal ones well into the 1880s; indeed Smith was not finally brought to trial until April 1888 when, by now a very old man, he was fined a nominal £10 and suffered the confiscation of his twenty-gallon still, his fermenting vessels and warming tub.

When Alfred Barnard undertook his epic visit to each of the 129 Scottish distilleries in the 1880s, he was quite often entertained by the son or grandson of someone who had founded the family connection with whisky in illegal circumstances. At *Dailuaine*, nestling in its enchanting glen in Strathspey, Barnard was shown the place where James Grant, known as James-am-Tuan or James of the Hills, the noted freebooter and outlaw, had his distilling stronghold. The ruins of one of the old smuggling bothies were clearly to be seen and the legend was still strong that the midnight wanderer might well observe

Glen Tanar looking north from the
lower slopes of Mount Keen. Part moorland, part arable. Glen Tanar at one time
had the finest fir forest in Aberdeenshire
but it was sold and cut down in the early
years of the nineteenth century.

Storm over Lochnagar looking from
Glen Tanar. Queen Victoria climbed
Lochnagar a week after her first visit to
Balmoral: 'Alas, nothing whatever to be
seen; and it was cold, wet and cheerless'.

evidence of their craft. The darker and wilder the night, the more likely you were to stumble upon the haunted bothy concealed in a cavern in a ravine through which one of the Dailuaine burns rushes. 'There the still-fires are seen weirdly sparkling like eyes of diamonds, and the ghosts of the departed smugglers busy at their ancient avocations. This discovery was made one winter's night by a shepherd who took shelter in a cleft of rock from the bleak winds and drifting snow, but he declined to say if he tasted the ghostly spirit.'

When they visited *Balmenach* in the Haughs of Cromdale, the sites of various illicit stills were pointed out to Barnard and his companions and on their arrival the proprietor's son, John MacGregor, took them on a conducted tour of the old smugglers' haunts. First they were shown a double-arched cavern, dug deep into the hillside some fifty yards from the distillery where at one time a band of smugglers had their headquarters. It was equipped with a subterranean spring into which was placed the worm which condensed the spirit. From the worm the spirit dripped into an earthenware jar about two feet high. The mash tun was an old wash-tub and the little copper still had stood on a furnace built from stones fallen from the walls of the cave. 'The place was totally dark and no light was ever permitted except that which came from the furnace fire. One night the revenue officers made a raid on the place and knowing the desperate men they had to deal with they were well armed. On their arrival they crept stealthily through the narrow entrance to the cave, following the informer who knew the place well.' The smugglers were unaware that they were about to be betrayed. Some were working the still, some sleeping the sleep of those who know they are justly breaking unjust laws. At that moment one of the smugglers opened the furnace door and the sudden flash of light revealed the excisemen. With great presence of mind the smuggler fired a pistol at the intruders and kicked the pipe away from the furnace. The cave filled with smoke and steam and the smugglers made a deft escape. Although none of the gang was caught, the still, the worm and the vessels were broken up and according to John MacGregor the betrayal finally put paid to smuggling in that area.

At *Inchgower* near Fochabers there were more smuggling stories. Alexander Wilson, the proprietor of this distillery which had originally been founded in 1824 by his great-uncle, showed them a farmhouse opposite the distillery where the noted smuggler McPherson had finally been captured by the law. He was bound for the seashore with several kegs of whisky concealed in trusses of straw in his cart when the excisemen pounced. Had he revealed the whereabouts of the illicit still at Aultmoor Glen whence the whisky came he might have been dealt with leniently, but he kept his mouth shut and took his secret to prison. The still was, like many another, secreted in a cavity in the hillside and the entrance was concealed with turf and heather. The water used

Cross Stone, Rowan Hill, Tarfside.

came from the same source now used legally by *Inchgower*.

Lochnagar was one of the many distilleries built by noted smugglers. *Fettercairn* distillery, near Laurencekirk, was originally established on the slopes of Cairn o'Mount in the heart of a notorious smuggling district; only in 1824 was it moved two miles down the hill to Fettercairn. Frequently Barnard came into direct contact with descendants of smugglers. When he visited *Grandtully* distillery near Aberfeldy, at that time the smallest in the United Kingdom, he was conveyed from the station by a coachman whose grandfather had been one of the most famous smugglers in the Aberfeldy neighbourhood. The still was concealed in a cave under the kitchen of a farmhouse. With the aid of a diverted spring, a flue carried seventy yards away to the chimney of the farmhouse and a confederate who tilled the farm, they managed to make whisky for years before being detected. It was an accomplice motivated by revenge and fired by the prospect of a substantial reward who betrayed them to the revenue officers. A midnight raid put paid to the operation. The four smugglers managed to escape and eventually made their way to America. Ten years later they returned to their native soil, settled down, married happily and became respectable members of the community: 'Our jolly driver quaintly reminded us that if his grandfather had not done this he would not have been there to drive us.'

Moving through the countryside of Ballinluig and Ballechin, they passed on to Logierait where another coach-driver regaled them with tales of the not at all distant past when in every secluded ben and shady corner smuggling bothies were at work. Among the Strath Tay smugglers, Barnard was told, were men of remarkable muscular power and shrewd audacity, the most famous being a Stewart whose last distillation was sold in Leith 'and was conveyed thither in a canopied cart, containing a caretaker muffled up as a patient (with an infectious disease) who managed thus to escape the prying curiosity of the excisemen and succeeded in disposing of the whisky at a high price'.

In the Ochil and Lomond Hills there once lay the noted distillery of *Auchtermuchty*. Indeed on the day of Barnard's visit, although he was shown around by one of the sons of the house, the works were still firmly in the hands of Alexander Bonthrone who had founded the distillery in 1829. Auchtermuchty, focal point of the fertile Howe of Fife, was at one time hotching with illicit distilleries and you could hardly move on the Ochil and Lomond hills without stumbling over a still. As late as the year 1828, Alexander Bonthrone's brother supplied the smugglers with malt. Carted away by night to the foot of the hills, it was collected under cover of darkness and dispersed to the caverns and hidey-holes where the *uisge* was distilled. Foremost among the smugglers was an Amazon known as Lady Miller and although Alexander Bonthrone, at that time the oldest practising distiller in Scotland if not

Invermark castle. The ruins lie thirteen miles north-west of Edzell; indeed it was an outpost to Edzell castle, the headquarters of the Lindsays of Glen Esk. Strategically it controlled the Fir Mounth, Mount Keen and the Forest of Birse passes. The tower dates from the 1520s. A seventeenth-century source described it thus: 'In Lochlie is the great and strong castle of Innermark upon the water of Northesk. It is very well peopled and upon any incursions of the Highland Katranes (for so those highland robbers are called) the Laird can, upon very short advertisement, raise a good number of well-armed prattie men, who seldom suffer any prey to goe out of their bounds unrecovered'.

in the world, told Alfred Barnard many a couthie story about her exploits. Barnard, alas, did not transcribe them.

Although all the illicit whisky produced on mainland Scotland had to be taken either on someone's back or by pony to the point of sale, in the islands the whisky roads for exporting the product to the mainland were marine. The leading whisky centre was and still is the island lying to the west of Kintyre known as Islay, which at one time had fourteen legal distilleries at work. There are still eight today making some of the most distinctive malts in Scotland. Whisky-making was the staple of island life and most of the population were involved in illicit activities. No evidence exists of the number of bothies, but there could have been few caves which did not contain tubs and casks and the apparatus necessary to convert barley into whisky.

In the island of Lewis illicit distilling was quite an open affair. In his *History of the Outer Hebrides* published in 1903, W.G. Mackenzie records that as late as 1827 smuggling was in full swing. 'It was no uncommon thing for even the Excise officers to be asked, when they were treated to a glass, which whisky they preferred, "Coll" or "Gress", both of which farms had celebrated stills.'

Up in Sutherland, the west-coast men were distilling enormous quantities of whisky in the early years of the nineteenth century and on the east coast round Helmsdale there were, so the Duke of Sutherland's factor James Loch was reliably informed, no less than 300 working stills. So much whisky was being produced that it had to be shipped out of the country south by sea. Loch wrote to the Home Office to complain that while the Stafford family were dispensing huge sums for the relief of the poor, 'these fellows are buying up all the barley in the county for the purpose of illicit distillation'.

In 1816 Loch's assistant, Patrick Sellar, had estimated that 25 per cent of the total rent of his Strathnaver estate depended on illicit distillation and the sale of black cattle. Indeed the rents had originally been calculated in the knowledge that they would almost certainly be paid from the profits of smuggling which was regarded as a calling as honourable as poaching.

Glen Tanar with its utilitarian estate
roads.

3 The Lawless and Illicit Banditti

Opposite Glen Callater, south east of Braemar, a bare desolate terrain with a brooding aspect of perpetual melancholy. The Glen is dominated by Lochnager and it provides the easiest point from which to scale that formidable protruberance. Glen Callater forms the northern end of the famous Jock's Road pass to Glen Doll.

The stories handed down by word of mouth always cast the smuggler in the role of hero. He or she is quick-witted, generous in defeat, good-humoured and eternally lucky. The excisemen are invariably depicted as plodding dim-wits, arriving in the wrong place at the wrong time, subjects of public mortification and universal derision.

On June 4, 1817, the *Aberdeen Journal* revealed to its readers the enterprising ruse adopted by a Kincardineshire woman who was one of the busiest distillers in a remote glen in the Highlands. A neighbour found out that the Excise knew what she was up to and an officer was on his way to apprehend her in the act. There was no time to dismantle her still and hide it, so in desperation the good wife lugged her infirm and bed-ridden husband to the door of the hut and put him in a chair so that he was blocking the entrance. When the exciseman arrived, he found the old woman standing over her apparently dying spouse and anointing his lips with a feather and some balm.

'For the love of Jesus,' she said with a melodramatic cry, 'if you are a clergyman come and pray for my dying husband.' The officer declined the invitation, saying that prayer wasn't one of his particular skills. 'In that case,' implored the woman, 'would you be kind enough to go as quickly as you can and send my neighbours to pray.' The officer agreed and departed. As soon as he was gone, the old man was dragged back to bed and distilling was resumed.

Dissembled mortality played a role in another popular story of the times. A smuggler who was not in the distilling business, but who indulged in the wholesale distribution of illicit spirit, got word that the gaugers were on their way to search his premises. As he had a big stock of full casks ready to be shipped, there seemed no escape from discovery. But once again invention saved the day. A tailor happened to be in the house and he agreed, in return for a suitable bribe, to be laid out on a table and covered with a white sheet. As the officer knocked on the door the women of the house broke into an impressive lament, the smuggler intoned piously from a Bible and invited the revenue men reverently into his house of mourning. Discountenanced, they made their excuses and left.

An even more preposterous tale comes from Kirkwall in the Orkney islands, where a smuggler called Magnus Eunson, by hobby a church elder, used to keep a stock of illicit whisky under the pulpit. On hearing that the church was to be searched for whisky, he had the casks removed to his house where he arranged them in the shape of a bier and covered them with a white cloth. When the officers burst into the room, Eunson was kneeling at the head of the bier with his Bible open and the rest of the family were keening lustily for the departed. 'Smallpox!' whispered one of the mourners to the nearest exciseman. They fled.

Many of the tales of thwarted detection have a quality reminiscent of the brothers Grimm. The one most repeated tells of the officer who stumbled upon a smuggler at work in his bothy.

'Did anyone see you coming here?' asked the smuggler.

'No one,' replies the officer.

'Then', says the smuggler reaching for an axe, 'no one will see you leave!'

Like the very best fairy tales, most of the whisky legends have been embellished in the telling until the participants stand like cardboard cutouts, the gaugers naive and gullible, the smugglers swift and wily. As in the Grimm canon, it is the little tailor who outwits the giant with ploys so simple they wouldn't fox a child.

If you are to believe what you are told, so much whisky was at one stage on the roads in the guise of funeral corteges and mortally sick patients being conveyed to the nearest fever hospital that the Excise must have begun to believe that the entire population of the Highlands was either dead or dying. So dim were the excisemen in any case that even a frail old lady could best them.

Ian Macdonald, late of the Inland Revenue, told many such stories to a meeting of the Gaelic Society of Inverness in 1887. 'Smuggling tales', he said, 'with their glamour and romance will ever remain part of our Scottish folklore and literature.' And he went on to relate how a poor woman was carrying a jar of whisky into Inverness from the hamlet of Abriachan eight miles away. As she neared the town, she was met by a kindly exciseman who insisted on relieving her of her burden.

'Oh, I am fainting,' groaned the old lady, 'give me just one mouthful out of the jar.' The officer allowed her to take a swig which she thereupon sprayed into his eyes. Blinded by the overproof spirit the officer, when he recovered his sight, found that the old lady had fled. And there are many more such tales which call upon a great suspension of disbelief if they are to be enjoyed to the full.

The parable of the cask and corkscrew is one such. Once, or perhaps one should say 'once upon a time', a cask of whisky was seized and conveyed by the guileless excisemen to an upper room in an inn at Bonar Bridge. While the officers sat contemplating their prize, a band of smugglers arrived and bribed the maid who was attending them to find out exactly where the cask was placed on the floor. So accurate were her observations that with unerring skill the smugglers were able to bore a hole through the floor and the bottom of the barrel. The spirit flowed out into an empty barrel below and the smugglers made off with it, leaving the silly excisemen guarding an empty barrel.

Another woman whose exploits became legendary was Ellen Cumming whose husband John Cumming, born in 1775, settled himself and his wife in the hamlet of Cardow near Knockando about the year 1813. Here, with several like-minded friends, he tilled the land and surreptitiously distilled whisky. As there were no inns near Cardow, the gaugers when they visited the area used to lodge at the Cummings' farmhouse. As soon as Ellen had prepared an evening meal for them, she would steal out into the farmyard and hoist a red flag over the steading to warn all her smuggling neighbours that their natural enemies had arrived on the scene. Once the red flag was spotted, the stills were dismantled and hidden. John Cumming legitimised his operation and took out a licence for *Cardow* in 1824.

Ellen, it was said, 'possessed the courage and energy of a man, and in devices and plans to evade the surveillance of the gaugers, no man or woman in the district could equal her.' But despite the superior nous of the smugglers and their wives, the gaugers weren't all that daft. Smugglers' tales told by smugglers are all of victories. Tales told by excisemen deal in statistics: stills confiscated, malt and spirit seized. In 1823 alone there were 14,000 detections, many of them effected unceremoniously and brutally.

No one was more successful in the prosecution of those who operated outwith the law than the Malcolm Gillespie I have already mentioned. His exploits might have gone unpublished had he not taken to uttering forged bills which, once they had come home to roost unredeemed, led to his trial and execution. It was said of Gillespie that 'he killed more of the enemy and seized more of their provisions and munitions of war than any ten of his brother officers.' An exciseman lived by his successes; his income came from a share of the sale price of any seizures he made. But Gillespie protested that paying for information and a band of men to assist him in his encounters with the smugglers far outweighed any remuneration he received. Owing £1,400, Gillespie sent a humble petition in 1826 to the Lords Commissioners of the Treasury. He described how in 28 years of service he had received no fewer than forty to fifty wounds in the discharge of his duty 'in detecting the lawless and illicit banditti'. Despite support from a prominent group of legal distillers, his petition fell on unimpressed ears.

The following year, accused of forging Treasury bills, he was confined in the Tolbooth in Aberdeen. The jury found him guilty and despite his zeal as an officer of the Revenue he was sentenced to be 'hanged by the neck upon a gibbet until he be dead'. Although Gillespie

Cardow, Knockando. Overlooking the river Spey the distillery draws its water from various springs in the hills. Its single malt is marketed under the name of Cardhu.

Scots pine near Archiestown southwest of Rothes. Late evening in midsummer.

was said to have looked suitably grave and melancholy on the receipt of this news, 'not a tear started – not a moan, nor even a sigh escaped him. He walked from the bar in silence with a steady step after bowing slowly and respectfully towards the court.'

While waiting for the reprieve which never came, Gillespie wrote his life and dying declaration, a document running to 19,000 words which is the most detailed account extant of the trials and hardships of an exciseman at the height of the era of illicit distilling.

From the east coast, where he had been so successful in stamping out a large part of the sea-borne contraband trade, Gillespie was appointed to the Skene Ride between the Dee and the Don in 1812. Skene itself is nine miles west of Aberdeen. In those days the parish held some 1,730 souls. A third of the land was moor and the northern part was hilly and bleak. More important for Gillespie was the fact that it not only contained a number of places where distilling could take place fairly circumspectly, but it also lay on one of the main whisky routes between the Highlands and Aberdeen which formed one of the principal markets for illicit spirit.

One of Gillespie's brighter ploys was to purchase ('at considerable expense') a bulldog which he trained to seize the noses of smugglers' horses and so throw the banditti into confusion. The dog proved its worth almost immediately. One February evening at Midmar Lodge, Gillespie stumbled on a gang of smugglers leading four horses laden with whisky. 'A desperate engagement ensued between Mr G. and these delinquents in which a deal of bloodshed occurred on both sides; and during the scuffle the dog was not idle. He seized the horses, one by one, till by tumbling some and others by dancing, in consequence of the pain occasioned by the hold the dog had of them by the nose, the ankers were all thrown from their backs.'

Attacked by bludgeons, sabres, pistols, sticks and stones, the intrepid Gillespie soldiered on sustaining broken limbs, scars and bruises by the score. The smugglers travelled in large bands, sometimes two dozen and more in number. These were not amateurs but professionals in a big way of business. One group in the Grampian hills possessed a fifty-gallon still 'with every apparatus necessary for the concern. It was so constructed that a person even of no ordinary penetration could scarcely be able to find it.' With a serjeant and a party of the Kincardine Volunteers summoned from Stonehaven for the occasion, Gillespie succeeded in locating the still, destroying 300 gallons and more of wash and low wines and demolishing the house in which the smugglers were carrying on their trade 'in violation of the laws of the country'. Gillespie reckoned that the output of the still was defrauding the government of about £100 duty a week, a substantial sum in those days.

Gillespie's largest haul took place near Inverurie in January 1824. He received intelligence that 'one of the most powerful and formidable gang of outlaws that ever graced the pages of delinquency' had assembled a large cargo of whisky which they proposed to smuggle to Aberdeen 'and if interrupted by any set of officers of excise whatever, they were determined to send them to the devil'. He lay in wait and it was not long before what Gillespie described as a thundering noise of carts was heard. There were ten in all guarded by about thirty smugglers. Gillespie ordered them to halt. When they refused, he shot one of the leading horses dead and a terrible conflict ensued.

'Bloody heads, hats rolling on the road, the reports of alternate firing and other noise, resembled more the battle of Waterloo than the interception of a band of lawless desperadoes.' At the end of the night Gillespie and his men found themselves in possession of 410 gallons of whisky, ten carts and fourteen horses.

These dramatic recitals of his skirmishes with the lawless men from the glens failed to soften the hearts of the judiciary and Gillespie was taken when his time came to the common place of execution in Aberdeen and duly suspended for all to see.

Gillespie was a night worker; all his seizures and encounters were made under cover of darkness, but in the more distant parts of the Highlands, illicit whisky was often moved from still to customer openly. Excisemen were thin on the ground and news of their movements was heralded well in advance. Joseph Mitchell, Chief Inspector and Superintendent of Highlands Roads and Bridges, noted how powerless the excisemen were in face of the popularity of the smugglers. 'There was a romance about it. The still was generally placed in some secluded spot, in the ravine of a Highland burn, or screened by waving birch and natural wood, so that the smoke of the fire could scarcely be observed. There were scouts placed around, often three or four savage-looking men, sometimes women and boys.'

It was to just such a scene that the London artist Robert Ronald M'Ian was taken about the year 1840 when he was collecting his impressions to illustrate *The Highlanders at Home*. That he was introduced into a smuggler's bothy by a clergyman and a factor, both local Justices of the Peace, reveals the ambivalent attitude of the gentry towards the smugglers. They might well be packed off to jail if caught, but as long as they kept out of the way of the gaugers they were a subject of picturesque amusement and a diversion for the visitor.

M'Ian happened to be in the Inverness area at the time and he applied to The Chisholm's factor, a Mr Robertson, for help. The Chisholm owned Erchless deer forest, a haunt of smugglers, none more diligent than Sandy MacGruar. 'If Sandy's out of jail', said the factor, 'you'll have no difficulty at all in seeing a bothy.' Messengers were despatched and the news came back, Sandy was at liberty and busy at the still. An appointment was made and with his sketching materials at the ready M'Ian, accompanied by the factor and the Rev.

Fraser of Erchless, was led into the dark retreat where Sandy plied his trade. The famous sketch was made and then the factor said, '*Nach eil dad agad, Alasdair?*' – 'Haven't you got a little something for us, Sandy?' Sandy foraged in the heather and unearthed a small keg; smuggler, artist and Justices toasted each other in the illicit *uisge*. 'What a fine haul the gaugers would have here,' said the minister, 'we'd better drink up and go!'

A character even more enterprising than Sandy was John Macdonald of Strathpeffer, of whom it was said with great local pride that the safest smuggling he ever did was during the time he was lodged in Dingwall jail. For many years after the Napoleonic wars, John kept two illicit bothies which he worked alternately. One was in Coire 'Bothain and the other at Leth-allt near Cnoc na Bainnse, both on the Heights of Strathpeffer. John was a loner and so never ran the risk of being betrayed by a confederate. But unfortunately a passing gamekeeper walking over the turf and bracken roof of the subterranean bothy at Coire 'Bhothain, fell through and confronted John tending his still. Being of an unfriendly disposition, he lodged information with the Dingwall court and John was given six weeks.

Mrs Macdonald walked to Dingwall and back every second day bringing a basket of food for her husband, but after a fortnight John made a pact with the warder. Each evening at dusk his cell door was unlocked and he slipped away over the hills to the small still at Cnoc na Bainnse. By daybreak he was back with a jar of whisky for the jailer, an arrangement of mutual advantage that occupied Macdonald industriously until he was officially released.

In some parts of the country the smugglers went about their business quite openly. Thomas Guthrie, who subsequently became a minister, recalled his boyhood days in Brechin. It would have been about 1818, when the Highland smugglers came and went with comparative immunity.

'They rode', he remembered, 'on Highland ponies, carrying on each side of their small, shaggy but brave and hardy steeds, a small cask or "keg" as it was called, of illicit whisky manufactured amid the wilds of Aberdeenshire, or the glens of the Grampians.'

During the day the smugglers halted and positioned themselves on some fairly high eminence where they could see who was coming and who was going and they had a keen eye for the excisemen. 'When night fell, every man to horse, descending the mountain only six miles from Brechin, they scoured the plains, rattled into the villages and towns, disposing of their whisky to agents they had everywhere; and, now safe, returned at their leisure, or often in a triumphal procession.'

The Rev. Guthrie recalled seeing a troop of thirty or so smugglers riding in broad daylight through the streets of Brechin having disposed of their whisky. 'They rode leisurely along, beating time with

The Lecht connects Strathdon with Strathavon and the road begins at Cock Bridge which is cut off from the outside world by winter snow and blizzards as regularly as Hogmanay. At the brink of the Conglass is the Well of the Lecht with an inscription, dated 1754, relating how the 33rd Regiment built the road from here to the Spey. The incongruous stone building, one of the few relics of industrial archeology in the area, dates from the days when manganese and ironstone mines were being worked in the vicinity. The ore was carried by ponies to smelting furnaces at Balnagown in Nethy Bridge.

Brechin Cathedral. The tower, surmounted by a spire, was built by Bishop Patrick about the year 1360. The round tower to the left is attached to the church and is thought to date from the tenth or eleventh centuries – it has affinities to the Celtic medieval towers found in Ireland.

Old peatbanks near Tomintoul.

their formidable cudgels on the empty barrels to the great amusement of the public and the mortification of the excisemen.' And to leave no one in doubt about the esteem in which the smugglers were held, the minister added, 'everybody, with few exceptions drank what was in reality illicit whisky – far superior to that made under the eye of the Excise – lords and lairds, members of Parliament and ministers of the gospel.' The toast of many a Highland laird as he raised his glass was 'cheap barley and success to smuggling'.

Even men of prominence in government employ, like Mitchell, could be relied upon to forget what they saw in the course of their travels. Many years after the event, Mitchell recalled an encounter with smugglers when riding, as a young man, up Glenmoriston before breakfast. Taking a turn in the road, he saw about 25 Highland ponies tied head to tail each carrying two kegs of whisky. A dozen or so men, some in kilts, all with bonnets, plaids and large bludgeons, were attending the whisky train. As Mitchell rode up, two of them fell back barring his way. 'It is a fine morning, sir' said one of them suspiciously. Mitchell returned the greeting. Then the man who had spoken turned to his companion and said in Gaelic, *'Cha ruig sibh leas – is e mac Mitchell, fear a' rathaid mhoir'* – You needn't mind; it is the son of Mitchell, the man of the high roads.'

Mitchell was then offered a dram and out came a round tin snuff-box without a lid. One of the smugglers filled it with whisky from a bottle in his side-pocket. After a little polite conversation and the downing of the dram, Mitchell moved on and as he passed each of the smugglers they touched their bonnets in deference both to his rank and his discretion.

Smugglers' bothies were a welcome source of comfort to travellers and sportsmen benighted on the hills. The naturalist Charles St John, in *The Wild Sports of the Highlands,* published in 1846, has left a vivid account of a remote bothy in the wild Glen Oykel region of Sutherland. St John pursued wildlife and shot it with an abandon which would make the present-day conservationist cringe with shock. One day in October 1833 he was out with a shepherd who produced irrefutable evidence that a pair of golden eagles were stealing his sheep. St John despatched the eagles as a favour, but even he had misgivings when he saw the magnificent birds lying dead. 'Eager as I had been to do the deed I could not look on the royal birds without a pang. But such regrets were now too late.' St John's main quarry on that occasion was a stag of extraordinary size which he had christened 'the Muckle Hart of Benmore' and on the following day, after trudging over the hills without catching any sight of the stag, it began to rain heavily. The gillie said he'd heard that there was a whisky bothy in the neighbourhood and when they saw a horse in the gloaming they knew it couldn't be far off. Then in the distance they heard the shrill treble of a fiddle.

'It's all right enough, sir,' said Donald, 'just follow the sound; it's that drunken deevil, Sandy Ross; ye'll never haud a fiddle frae him, nor him frae a whisky-still.' Up to their waists in ice-cold water they staggered across a dark mountain burn, holding their guns high over their heads and then scrambling up the bank they came to what looked like a mere hole in the bank. 'The hole was partially closed by a door woven of heather and looking through it we saw a sight worthy of Teniers. On a barrel in the midst of the apartment – half hut, half cavern – stood aloft, fiddling with all his might, the identical Sandy Ross, while round him danced three unkempt savages; and another figure was stooping, employed over a fire in the corner where the whisky-pot was in full operation.'

There ensued a wild party and St John had 'disturbed visions of strange orgies in the bothie, and of my sober Donald exhibiting curious antics on top of the tub . . . there is no doubt that when daylight awoke me, the smugglers and Donald were all quiet and asleep, far past my efforts to rouse them, with the exception of one who was still able to tend the fire under the large black pot.' There would have been no question of St John ever revealing the whereabouts of the bothy to the law. To him, as to any gentlemen of his day, illicit distilling was just another harmless aberration of the feckless Highlander.

If ever a defence was needed of smuggling, then no remark is more quotable than that of Dr John Mackenzie of Inverewe, whose nephew Osgood Mackenzie created the famous west-coast Highland gardens now owned by the National Trust. 'My father', wrote Dr John proudly in his manuscript 'Highland Memories', 'never tasted any but smuggled whisky and when every mortal that called for him – they were legion daily – had a dram instantly poured into him, the ankers of whisky emptied yearly must have been numerous indeed. I don't believe my mother or he ever dreamed that smuggling was a crime.'

Everyone the young John Mackenzie met, even the clergy 'either made, bought, sold or drank cheerfully, smuggled liquor'. Excisemen were planted in central stations as a terror to evil-doers, but they seemed to stay for life in the same localities and 'report said they and the regular smugglers of liquor were bosom friends and that they even had their ears and eyes shut by blackmail pensions from the smugglers.'

But the friendly resident gaugers were soon afterwards replaced by 'riding officers', zealous men like the troublesome Gillespie, and squads of what John Mackenzie described as 'horrid coastguard sailors with long, iron-pointed walking sticks for poking wherever earth seemed to have been lately disturbed'. The peaceful days of smuggling were ended for 'these rascals ransacked every unenclosed bit of country within their limits each month'.

Glen Mark at the foot of Mount Keen
near the Queen's Well, looking north to
the summit of Couternach.

4   Temptations Too Strong To Resist

Opposite Antler, Corryhabbie burn.
Only stags grow antlers; the stag calf
produces his first set when he is about a
year old. Antlers are ast between March
and May and re-grown each year. During the growing period the new antlers
are covered with velvet which eventually
rubs off. There are 2½ million acres of
deer forest in the Highlands; much of
the ground is over 2000 feet and the red
deer is the best adapted animal to use it.
In a hard winter many deer perish and
many hinds lose their calves; bad
weather brings them down from the hills
and they are adept at avoiding blizzards.
The red deer population is kept at
acceptable levels by culling. The close
season is from October 21 to June 30 for
stags and February 16 to October 20 for
hinds. Deer stalking in the Highlands
attracts sportsmen from all over the
world; the annual cull is about 16,000
stags and 20,000 hinds.

The running war between the smugglers and the government, particularly in the heart of the Highlands, had become so vicious in the first
two decades of the last century that landowners, a powerful force in
those days of huge estates, found themselves under increasing pressure to curb the illicit activities of their tenants. The authority of the
laird was absolute and autocratic but it did not seem to extend very
enthusiastically to the stamping out of smuggling; had someone like
the Duke of Atholl wished to banish illicit distillation from his broad
acres it could have been accomplished merely by the raising of a finger.

Feudalism was as rife as pauperism in these parts and the compul-
sory clearance of the people from populous glens was rampant in the
Grampians long before James Loch and Patrick Sellars began their
systematic depopulation of Sutherland. As you walk the empty glens
and straths or wander along the old overgrown whisky roads, it is right
to remember why they are so empty. Much of this area was at one time
heavily populated; the land now thick with bracken grew corn and kail
and cattle grazed on the slopes. The breakdown began with the arrival
of the sheep. Small farmers were driven from fertile land in the valleys
to stony ground where they could barely scratch a living. After the
sheep came an even more profitable innovation. Huge deer forests
were created to increase rents and the remaining peasantry were
encouraged to depart.

The word 'forest' to English ears conjures up visions of noble oaks
and bluebell-carpeted glades, but the Highland deer forests were more
frequently than not treeless upland acres. The great Caledonian Forest
which once extended, in the words of a Victorian naturalist, 'from Glen
Lyon and Rannoch to Strathspey and Strathglass and from Glencoe
eastwards to the Braes of Mar' and was rich in oak, birch, alder, pine
and hazel, had fallen early on to the destructive hand of man. Besides
plundering, the Vikings were keen on burning forests either to drive
out fugitives or for sheer pleasure.

The Norsemen were followed by indigenous gangsters like the Earl
of Badenoch nicknamed the Wolf of Badenoch, who, had he been alive
today, would doubtless be under psychiatric observation. Having set
fire to a large part of the landscape, he descended on Forres and burnt
it down. If one is to believe Shakespeare, much of the moorland in

Ballindalloch Lodge, near *Glenfarclas*.
Ballindalloch castle itself dates from the
early sixteenth century and is not open to
hoi polloi. Here successive lairds created
the most perfect herd of Aberdeen
Angus cattle in the country.

Trees in Craigellachie forest.

those parts was already fairly bleak. Connoisseurs of Holinshed will recall that it was on their way to put paid to King Duncan at Forres that Macbeth and Banquo met the weird sisters on their blasted heath. The Wolf visited his wrath the following year on Elgin (noted now for the distilleries of *Glenlossie, Linkwood* and *Miltonduff*) and in 1390 burnt down the Cathedral of St Giles, the hospital and eighteen manses of the canons and chaplains.

Although in troubled times many woods were felled to smoke out thieves and rebels, by far the greatest destruction to the natural beauty of the landscape came from charcoal burning and the demand for wagonloads of timber for the smelting industries of the south. After the failure of the Jacobite rebellion of 1715, many forfeited estates were sold for their timber, but even earlier than that the lairds were disposing of their heritage. In 1728 Sir James Grant sold 60,000 of his trees to fire the furnaces of England and the Lowlands, and in 1786 the Duke of Gordon sold the timber of Glenmore Forest to an English smelting company. The famous Caledonian pine forest of Rothiemurchus was reduced year after year by tree-felling and the arrival of sheep-farming added to the destruction. In 1848, the year that Victoria and Albert first visited Balmoral, Strathfarrer was cleared to make way for sheep and it is said twelve miles of birch, pine and oak were fired to provide the pasture for the four-legged 'eaters of men'.

So by the time the vogue for deer began, what little forest remained had diminished to a few patches on the bald head of the land, and the population too was being ruthlessly cut down to size. The history of Glen Tilt is typical of the way in which once well-farmed land was turned into an empty wilderness punctuated only by the echo of autumnal gunfire as a shooting party from the south bagged their quota of deer. Glen Tilt itself is only one of the many glens which bites into the Grampians. It is, however, a place of remarkable beauty leading up to moorland and eventually on to Deeside and Balmoral.

In 1846, some sixty years after it had been cleared, Robert Somers, investigating the distress caused by the failure of the Scottish potato crop, set foot in the Glen which had at the time been closed to the public by its owner the Duke of Atholl.

'I took some delight', recorded Somers, 'in traversing the old roads, and in tracing out the sites of the numerous dwelling-places with which the glen has at one time been thickly studded. Formerly a seat of rural townships, Glen Tilt is now a scene of utter desolation.' And so it remains to this day.

At one time there were probably four or five hundred people living there. Each family possessed a patch of arable land and the hill was held for communal benefit. 'The people', wrote Somers, 'enjoyed full liberty to fish in the Tilt, an excellent salmon river; and the pleasures and profits of the chase were nearly as free to them as to their chief.' But

Cheese press at Glen Esk Folk Museum.

Old cheese press and ruined house, Whigginton, Glen Esk.

then the Duke decided to move deer onto the land. He built a high stone dyke at the head of the Glen and the people were forbidden to go beyond it. It had long been their custom in the summer to take the cattle up to a higher glen watered by the river Tarf but this annual migration was now deemed to be trespass. As the deer multiplied they began destroying the crops in the glen. Gradually the deer forest was extended 'and gradually the marks of cultivation were effaced, till the last man left the glen and the last cottage became a heap of ruins. The same devastation which William the Conquerer and the early Norman kings spread over the plains of Hampshire in the eleventh and twelfth centuries, was thus reproduced at the end of the eighteenth in this quiet Highland valley.'

The land which could have supported a thousand people became a playground for sportsmen. Similar devastations were re-enacted all over the Grampians. Turf huts fell back into the ground and stone walls were tumbled as the Highlands were turned into private pleasure parks for the pursuit of game. Those who had the tenacity to remain where they and their forefathers were born were hedged with restrictions. As Somers wrote, 'to kill a fish in the stream or a wild beast upon the hills is a transportable offence. Even to travel through the fenceless forests is a crime and paths which have linked hamlets with hamlets for ages past have been shut and barred.'

The families who were cleared owned six or seven cows, a couple of horses and perhaps up to eighty sheep. Even in times of hardship, much of it self-inflicted by indolence and poor farming practice, they could survive. If a crofter fell ill his barley continued to grow and his cows to chew the cud and produce milk. But the same man, when dispossessed of his land, became a charge on the parish. As the people were removed so all semblance of prosperity disappeared with them. In the thirty years between 1801 and 1831 the population of Blair Atholl, for instance, fell by 500.

A thriving community creates work; depopulation leaves only solitude and picturesque beauty. 'The clearance and dispersion of the people', recorded Somers, 'is pursued by the proprietors as a settled principle, as an agricultural necessity, just as trees and brushwood are cleared from the wastes of America or Australia; and the operation goes on in a quiet business-like way, that neither excites the remorse of the perpetrators nor attracts the sympathy of the public.'

The huge Braemar and Atholl forests were soon joined by deer forests at Glenfeshie, Ardverikie and the immense desolation of Black Mount. As the railways began to push north, so the rents of sporting estates, now a comfortable overnight journey from London, rose to new and gratifying heights. A series of articles in *The Times* in 1883, a decade when every successful industrialist in England had his ambitions fixed fashionably on the ownership of a Highland estate, pointed

Above and opposite Old lime kiln at
Arsallery. Lime was used widely in building and to counteract the natural acidity
of the soil. Arsallary, north of Tarfside,
was once a flourishing village; now only
the sheep remain.

out that the number of sporting properties was unhappily limited. 'As landlords lose money or incur risks and trouble by their sheep-farms', it added comfortingly, 'they will naturally throw suitable grazings into forests, which will yield them larger rentals without any trouble at all. But a deer forest implies the appropriation of a great surface of country, and half-a-dozen of the millionaires who can indulge in first-class forests will find themselves unpleasantly crowded in a district that might have been cut up into some scores of grouse-shootings; so that great parts of the wild north are likely to be locked up by a close corporation of stalkers, into which admission can only be gained by money and patience.'

These were shameless times and the writer showed no embarrassment as he dismissed the effects of this speculative land-grabbing. 'I say nothing on the economic side of the question and the possible national loss of sweeping off the sheep that have supplied our markets; all I assert is that the present tendency of the land movement is to increase the holdings of great monopolists and thus diminish the area left available for others . . . Should deer-stalking become a fashion among American and Australian capitalists, we may even see a "corner" in moors and forests and a return of the wonderful profits of thirty years ago.'

At that time, eleven individuals (the Dukes of Sutherland, Atholl, Argyll, Richmond, Lady Matheson of Lews, Sir Charles Ross, A. Matheson Esq. and Lord Lovat) owned between them *4.2 million acres.* In English terms it was as if eleven people owned between them the whole of Berkshire, Oxfordshire, Somerset, Surrey, Staffordshire, Warwickshire and Wiltshire. Not even the staunchest supporter of private enterprise would maintain that a situation where eleven people controlled over a fifth of the land mass of Scotland was a healthy one for either the economy or the people. The depressing chronicle of land alienation and misuse makes one look upon the clandestine distiller with a kindlier eye. He despoiled no forests, cleared no glens; he didn't create a monopoly of the land for his own interests or lock up whole landscapes for his personal pleasure. The product of his skill gave fleeting enjoyment at minimal cost to those who could afford it. Apart from depriving the crown of what many right-thinking men regarded as a damnable imposition and leading the revenue men a prolonged and dangerous dance, smuggling was a relatively innocuous pastime.

But, as I said, feeling in Westminster began to build up against the owners of the small stills and pressure was exerted on the owners of the land on which these stills were sited. No nobleman found himself more pressured than the Duke of Richmond and Gordon whose territory stretched from one side of Scotland to the other. Fort William at the head of Loch Linnhe on the west coast had once been named Gordonsburgh and the Gordon policies marched east to the Moray Firth and south to Glenlivet. Macdonalds, Macintoshes and Macphersons owed fealty to the Gordons and their sway in Aberdeen and Banff was absolute.

Scattered over their hereditary lands were hundreds of illicit stills, the most renowned being in Glenlivet. The waters of the Livet flow north from the Ladder Hills and into the Avon and whether it was the water itself, the large number of pure springs to be found there or the artistry of the local people, the whisky that came over the hills to the south from Glenlivet was justly famous. George IV, when he resorted to whisky, would have nothing on his table but Glenlivet, and his fondness for this illicit spirit made a royal mockery of the laws which its production contravened.

When the King came on his second visit to Scotland in 1822 the *opéra bouffe* proceedings were stage-managed by Sir Walter Scott who was received on board the royal yacht in the Roads of Leith by the beaming Hanoverian monarch.

'What!' exclaimed His Majesty, 'Sir Walter Scott! – The man in Scotland I most wish to see! Let him come up.' As soon as Scott had gained the deck, he made a small speech on behalf of the ladies of Edinburgh, presented the King with a silver cross and then joined George in a bumper of Glenlivet. Having asked the King if he might keep the glass in which the toast had been drunk, Scott put it for safekeeping in his coat pocket but subsequently sat on it, a moment of historic pain. 'His scream and gesture', recorded his literary executor, 'made his wife conclude that he had sat down on a pair of scissors or the like: but very little harm had been done except the breaking of the glass, of which he alone had been thinking.'

The King took up his residence in the Palace of Holyrood and consumed more of the illicit stuff. For that we have the word of Elizabeth Grant of Rothiemurchus: 'Lord Conynghame, the Chamberlain, was looking everywhere for the pure Glenlivet whisky; the King drank nothing else. It was not to be had out of the Highlands. My father sent word to me – I was the cellarer – to empty my pet bin, where was whisky long in the wood, long in uncorked bottles, mild as milk, and the true contraband *goût* to it. The whisky and fifty brace of ptarmigan all shot by one man went up to Holyrood House and were graciously received and made much of.'

If whisky distilled on his lands by one of his tenants found such favour with the King, who was the Duke of Gordon to put a stop to it? But both houses of Parliament in the 1820s were bending their attentions to a possible reform in the fiscal regulations and strong representations were made to the proprietors of Scottish estates to use their influence in preventing the law from being so successfully and so flagrantly broken. It was a daunting task. Indeed when the Duke of Gordon's factor was asked for a list of all the tenants engaged in distilling in the Glenlivet area, he found it both easy and difficult, for there were few who were not active in the illicit trade, either at source or somewhere along the line.

Eventually the Duke made a statement to the House of Lords in which he claimed, stretching truth a little, that the Highlanders were born distillers, whisky was their beverage from time immemorial and with the duty as high as it was, the temptations to make and sell it illegally were too strong for them to resist. But, said the Duke, if Parliament would frame an Act which enabled the Highlanders to manufacture legal whisky without having to pay an unreasonable duty, then he and his fellow proprietors would do their best to put down smuggling and encourage the creation of legal distilleries.

The following year an Act to Eliminate Illicit Distilling was passed and George Smith of Upper Drumin, with the encouragement of the Duke of Gordon, took out the new licence of £10 and began distilling legal whisky on which he paid a duty of 2s 3d a gallon. On the site of his old illicit bothy at Minmore he built the first legal distillery in Glenlivet.

But it was to be quite a few years before his neighbours became reconciled to his move to legality. As George Smith recalled in later life, 'I was warned by my civil neighbours that they meant to burn the new distillery to the ground and me in the heart of it.' The Laird of Aberlour, to encourage farmer Smith, presented him with a ten-guinea pair of pistols which were never out of Smith's reach. 'I got together two or three stout fellows for servants, armed them with my pistols, and let it be known everywhere that I would fight for my place to the last shot.' Threats, according to Smith, were not the only weapons used. 'In 1825 a distillery which had just started near the Banks o'Dee at the head of Aberdeenshire was burnt to the ground with all its outbuildings and appliances, and the distiller had a very narrow escape from being roasted in his own kiln. The riding officers of the revenue were the mere sport of the smugglers and nothing was more common for them to be shown a still at work and then coolly defied to make a seizure.'

Even as late as 1834, there were just under 700 detections of illicit stills and the isolated glens and roads which connected them with their markets on the coast and further south were the continuing scene of pitched battles with excisemen and the troops they frequently called to their aid. Hundreds of gallons of illicit whisky continued to be transported into the towns by bands of increasingly desperate smugglers. The castles of Corgarff and Braemar were refurbished at a cost of £1,200 in 1827 to serve as a base for the Light Dragoons who came to be known as 'The Terror of the Smugglers'. The excise courts at Keith and Grantown were dealing with a steady stream of smugglers queuing up to pay their £20 fines. Our old and unfortunate friend, Malcolm Gillespie, made in 1827, the year of his execution, what he described to

Braemar castle. The castle stands on a bluff overlooking the Dee. Built in 1628 by John Erskine, seventh Earl of Mar, as a hunting lodge, it was attacked and burnt in 1698 by the Farquharsons and after the failure of the acobite rising in 1715 it was garrisoned by government troops. The War Office who leased the fabric for a 99-year period added a curtain wall similar to the one at Corgarff. Like Corgarff it was used until well into the nineteenth century as a headquarters for the suppression of smuggling.

The Braemar Gathering was first held in 1832 and Queen Victoria gave it the royal seal of approval in 1848. Since then the royals have seldom been absent and each September about 50,000 visitors turn up to watch the Queen and her beartaned family as they settle down for a day of piping, dancing, tossing the caber and throwing the hammer.

The descendants of the Duffdefiance squatters. A family, evicted from Glenbuchat estate in the nineteenth-century for persistent illicit distilling, moved to this lonely spot on the Ladder. Fay met their descendants, some 30 of them, having a reunion barbecue to commemorate the spirited enterprise of their forebears. Some of the family still live in the valley. Eviction for smuggling did more to stamp it out than any government legislation and a determined landowner with unlimited powers could, if he so wished, run anyone off his property.

In Tiree the Duke of Argyll decreed that every tenth man caught illicitly distilling should be evicted. As there were over 150 cases of illicit distilling on the Tiree estates during the year 1800–1801 this meant that some fourteen tenants and their dependants were removed. If one examines the reasoning behind the evictions they appear in a less draconian light. There were many years of such meagre harvests that the grain was needed to feed the people, not intoxicate them. Sir James Grant of Strathspey wrote to his factor in November 1800: 'We in the county of Inverness are taking effectual measures to suppress the illicit distillation which is so highly criminal at a time when grain is so much wanted for the food of the inhabitants'.

Rowan Hill. Is this pile of stones all that remains of an illicit distillery? Or was it just a shepherd's *bothan* or the home of some early Celtic hermit or misanthrope? Locals favour the whisky connection.

a friend in Edinburgh as 'one of the most extensive seizures ever captured in the north of Scotland of the very best Glenlivet'. As Gillespie pointed out, 'the new Distilling Laws and the indulgence to Legal Distillation has in a very trifling degree reduced whisky in this quarter as our North Country Gentry will not drink the Large Still Whisky.'

But moonlight whisky was on the wane. Despite the risks which George Smith had been faced with in Glenlivet, a dramatic rise in legal distilleries had begun. Over the years the excitement went out of smuggling and one by one the illicit stills fell in. Old men, enthusiasts of the worm, became arthritic and could no longer work o' nights. Young men did not spring up to take their place. The pleasures and excitements of illegality gave way to the dull and duty-paid. There is no better description of how that happened than the one given by the late Sir Robert Bruce Lockhart in his book *Scotch*.

Sir Robert's maternal great-grandfather, James Macgregor, who came from Tomintoul, started a farm at Balmenach in the Haughs of Cromdale. He and his two brothers had been engaged in illicit distillation in Tomintoul and probably left because they found the attentions of the excisemen becoming more and more tedious. Macgregor hacked his farm out of peat, bog and heather and quietly continued his distilling. Not long after the passing of the Act of 1823 he was paid a visit by the nearest excise officer.

Their talk was friendly and began with a generous dram of pure malt whisky. When these preliminaries were finished to the satisfaction of both men, the excise officer mentioned shyly that he had his duty to perform and had better have a look round. Out went the two men to inspect the farm. All went well until they came to a rough stone building with a mill-wheel and a mill-lade by its side.

'What will that be?' asks the excise officer.

'Oh', says my great-grandfather, 'that'll just be the peat-shed.'

Nothing more was said and the two men went back to the house for another dram and a talk about the crops and the prospects for the harvest. Then as the gauger took his leave, he said quietly:

'If I were you, Mr Macgregor, I'd just take out a licence for yon peat-shed.'

Balmenach became legal in 1824.

Corgarff castle in the Spring.

5 A Small Tremour of the Earth

Opposite The Queen's Well. 'We mounted our ponies a little after three and rode down Glen Mark stopping to drink some water out of a very pure well called the White Well and crossing the Mark several times. As we approached the Manse of Loch Lee the glen widened and the old castle of Invermark came out extremely well and, surrounded by woods and corn-fields in which the people were shearing, looked most picturesque' – thus Queen Victoria described her second great expedition with Prince Albert to Fettercairn in September 1861. The royal party travelled in double dog carts and on their way to Fettercairn the Queen and her Consort lunched with Lord Dalhousie in Glenmark Cottage at the foot of the Ladder burn. Within a few weeks Albert was dead, a victim of typhoid. Lord Dalhousie raised a memorial to commemorate the royal visit to the well in the form of an imperial crown nearly twenty feet high. On the basin are inscribed the words: 'Rest traveller, on this lonely green and drink and pray for SCOTLAND's Queen'.

In the sixty years between 1824, when James Macgregor made *Balmenach* legal, and 1884, when the Crofters' Act was passed, almost seventy new distilleries were set up. So that means that the majority of the 117 malt distilleries in Scotland have been operating for over a hundred years, many more for a century and a half, a handful since the eighteenth century. They are the most tangible piece of continuity, the most obvious manifestation of industrial archaeology that you are likely to see on a Highland jaunt. There are no breweries left in the Highlands today and yet at one time there were plenty. Iron-smelting died out a century ago. Grain mills, threshing mills, linen mills, bleachworks, waulk and gig mills are all gone. Where slateworks and quarries, flour and fulling and jute mills, ropeworks and fish-curing houses have been abandoned, you'll still find the local distillery at work. They have persisted where new-fangled inventions have come and gone. Over fifty of the distilleries you can see today were well established before the first railway sleeper was laid in Scotland. The Victorian stations at Craigellachie, Aberlour, Dailuaine, Knockando and Ballindalloch are closed now and the old railway lines have been torn up. The steam trains came and went; the distilleries remain.

It would be wrong to pretend that whisky is made in exactly the same way that it was in the days of the smugglers, but there are few distilleries operating today where you cannot put your hand on the past. Here are the old stables, the malting floors, the kilns, the still-rooms, the cooperage which at one time gave work to most of the able-bodied men in the vicinity. The copper stills may have been replaced four or five times in the last hundred years and more but they retain the shape they had in the days when there were such people about as harness-makers, farriers, wheelwrights, fletchers, smiths and lime-burners.

To take a whisky road in the Highlands is to step back into the past. There have been, of course, many changes. The horse has been pensioned off, water-power has been replaced by electricity, coal by propane gas and malting is done in centralised complexes. But the heart of the matter, the transubstantiation of a mash of barley into a clear and fiery liquid, is the same now as it was in the days of Burns. The wash is heated, the vapours ascend, the drops of whisky form. Every year nearly half a million visitors are shown how it's done – a tradition of curiosity which goes back into Victorian times. So let's go back and see how different whisky distilling was a hundred years ago. We'll take a guided tour round a distillery which has enjoyed royal patronage for over 130 years. *Lochnagar*, which takes its name from a mountain apostrophised by Byron, lies less than a mile away from Balmoral where Victoria and Albert played out their brief Highland idyll.

You have taken the overnight train from King's Cross in London to Aberdeen and perhaps booked into the Imperial Hotel opposite the station in Stirling Street. Being a person of taste, you have chosen the Imperial because it is the only establishment in the city expressedly built from the foundation as a first-class hotel. Patronised by Their Royal Highnesses the Duke of Edinburgh, the Prince and Princess Christian and Duke Leopold, it has magnificent lavatories and no stairs to climb. Although close to the station, it is 'entirely removed from the disturbing influence of the railway and the dangerous and deleterious effect of promixity to the smoke and steam of the trains'. Not only that: by means of air shafts and charcoal frames, the drainage system is perfect. A good point that; it is but a few years since the Prince Consort fell victim to the drains of Windsor and succumbed to typhus.

From Aberdeen to Ballater by rail is only 43½ miles. There are five trains a day and if you are of the quality you will purchase a first-class ticket for 6s 10d. The route, which for most of the way follows the Dee, is delightfully picturesque with many noble buildings to be seen amid the trees. Past Banchory House and the Deeside Hydropathic Establishment with its turreted tower on the far side of the river, past the House of Durries, past Park House with its metal bridge across the Dee, and Crathes Castle, residence of Sir J. H. Burnett of Leys, Bart, a building in the Flemish style which rises into a cluster of turrets, chimneys and peaked gables.

From here the ground begins to rise to the Grampians. Seventeen miles from Aberdeen and we steam into Banchory where the Dee is joined by the dark and angry-looking burn of the Feugh. From here the Slug Road crosses Cairn-mon-earn to Stonehaven and the Cairn o'Mount pass to Fettercairn can be tackled. The summit of Cairn-mon-earn commands a magnificent view of the sea and the Howe o' the Mearns as well as the whole Deeside Valley.

After Banchory the line leaves the riverside and curves northward toward the Hill of Fare from whose summit you can view the castellated mansion of Dunecht, seat of the Earl of Crawford. At Lumphanan the parliamentary road strikes off to Alford and Huntly and if you broke your journey you might observe the cairn which legend claims to cover the mortal remains of Macbeth. Another more likely legend says the king who murdered sleep is interred in the royal sepulchre on Iona. Take your choice.

Crathes castle. The gardens of this sixteenth century castle, 14 miles west of Aberdeen and two miles east of Banchory, cover about six acres within the walls and are subdivided by huge yew hedges planted in the reign of Queen Anne. The gardens which are known to bontanists all over the world are six in number and feature rare plants and shrubs from South Africa, California, India, the Himalayas and Chile.

Ruins of a hospice near the top of Cairn
o' Mount. Such 'spittals' which would
have had a chapel attached to them are
perpetuated in place names like Spittal
of Glenshee and Spittal of Muick.

The Fungle at Birse castle. The Fungle is
still a well marked track from Aboyne to
Glen Esk (see walks)

On to Aboyne and the multi-turreted Aboyne Castle seat of the Marquis of Huntly. Alight here and you will encounter a delicate wooded glen with waterfalls, the Fungle, which will take you over to the Forest of Birse and the old whisky road to Brechin. The road up the riverside passes the mouth of Glen Tanar, famed for its residual Scots pines, part of the old Caledonian Forest. Great changes in the glen were inaugurated by W. Cunliffe Brooks Esq., a millionaire who became Laird of Glentanar in 1859. A consuming passion for construction and limitless wealth enabled him to retain a permanent private army of masons and joiners who erected cottages, churches, lodges and chapels in a frenzy of enthusiasm. The mansion-house in the glen was turned into a Victorian gentlemen's dream of feudal splendour. The Brooks style was Gothic with Hammer House of Horror overtones. The antler-hung Chapel of St Lesmo (pews lined with deerskin) is, as Michelin says, well worth a detour.

From Aboyne the line runs due west on the land of the Marquis; fine views of forest land picturesquely broken with rocks are laid before the passenger. Passing through a tunnel, a more open range of country appears. 'The view', wrote Queen Victoria in her diary on September 19, 1859, 'is more magnificent than can be described, so large and yet so near everything seemed, and such seas of mountains with blue lights, and the colour so wonderfully beautiful.' Then on across the Muir of Dinnet and the distant prospect of Lochnagar clad in perennial snow. Close by is Ballatrich, the farmhouse where the eight-year-old Byron convalesced after an attack of scarlet fever. Lochnagar made a profound impression upon him. 'Oh for the crags that are wild and majestic,' he wrote, 'The steep frowning glories of dark Loch na Garr!'

After crossing the Tullich water by the iron railway bridge, the train puffs slowly into the terminus at Ballater. Opposite the station is the gaunt granite edifice of the Albert Hall, erected by Mr Gordon in memory of the departed Consort. Mindful perhaps of the Prince's abrupt demise, the liberal proprietor of Ballater, Colonel Farquharson of Invercauld, has given the small town a supply of pure fresh water and an extensive drainage system.

In May and autumn, when the widowed Queen spent two months in residence at Balmoral, it was her custom to take a drive morning and afternoon and a fresh pair of horses was kept for her carriage at the Invercauld Arms in Ballater. If on this spring day in 1888 you have just arrived on the train from Aberdeen bent on visiting *Lochnagar* distillery as Alfred Barnard has, then you must be among the first out of the station to secure a seat on the coach. If there's room on the box seat beside the driver, climb up at once, for the drive to Balmoral is, in Barnard's words, superb 'and upon a fine day the scene presented to the eye is not one easily forgotten'.

The road to Braemar and Balmoral follows the north bank of the

Balmoral castle.

Game larders.

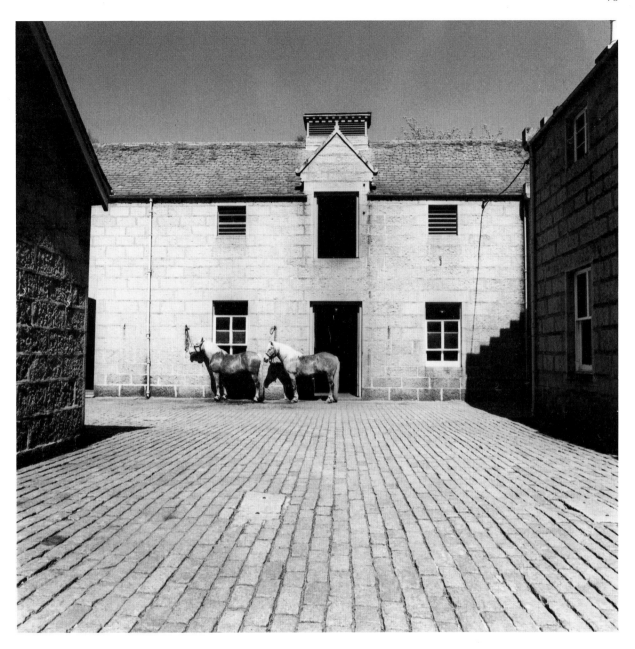

The special breed of ponies used to bring
deer carcases down from the hills.

Decorative deer.

Target deer.

Despite the appalling weather they encountered on their first visit to the western Highlands both Victoria and Albert fell deeply in love with everything they saw. In 1847 when the royal couple cruised up the west coast and stayed at Ardverikie on Loch Laggan it poured incessantly, but Victoria praised 'the view from the windows . . . though obscured by rain it is very beautiful and extremely wild'. Albert wrote to Baron Stockmar describing how 'whenever we stir out we come home almost frozen and always wet to the skin'. And that was in August! Fired with the idea of possessing a holiday retreat in the Highlands they settled, at the suggestion of their Physician in Ordinary, Sir James Clark, on the drier eastern side of Scotland. James Giles, an Aberdeen artist, was commissioned to make sketches of the countryside along the Dee. The Queen was enchanted and when the estate of Balmoral came on the market she acquired the lease unseen. In September 1848 the royal yacht *Victoria and Albert* bore the court north. There was a triumpant progress from Aberdeen along Deeside through mile after mile of floral arches to what was to become the beloved Balmoral. The Aberdeen architect, William Smith, was commanded to Balmoral where, under Albert's enthusiastic guidance plans were set in motion to create a residence large enough to accomodate the court. By 1856 Victoria recorded in her *Journal*: 'Every year my heart becomes more fixed in this dear paradise and so much more now that *all* has become my dearest Albert's *own* creation, own work, own building, own laying out, as at Osborne, and his great taste and the impress of his dear hand have been stamped everywhere'.

By August 1860 only the Prince Consort's model dairy remained unfinished. Balmoral was almost complete. Before returning south to Osborne and her imminent and catastrophic widowhood the Queen wrote . . . 'Oh! those beloved hills – that pure air – those dear people – all must be left tomorrow. But I am truly grateful for what I have enjoyed'.

river, passing by the woods of Craigendarroch. Six miles up the road is the shooting box of the Prince of Wales; a little beyond is the village of Crathie with its plain, box-like kirk in which Queen Victoria worships, and across the river is Balmoral, if not the most beautiful castle in the Highlands certainly the most famous. 'Here', wrote the deferential Barnard, 'is the chosen retreat of our beloved Queen, and it would be difficult to find a more beautiful spot. On one side a wooded haugh slopes gently down from Craig Gowan's shaggy side to the margin of the River Dee, on the borders of which the noble castle is built; on the other are ranged battlements of hills with glimpses of magnificent scenery, while eastward is to be seen the Rock of Oaks and the pine-covered hills of Invercauld.'

At this time, the estate of Balmoral consisted of 10,000 acres and a deer forest of 30,000 acres. The castle was designed by Albert to house up to 120 residents and the construction of this Highland *Schloss* was entrusted to the city architect of Aberdeen, William Smith. It was a substantial and stately palace that Albert had wrought, with plenty of everything: 180 windows opening onto the romantic Deeside views, 67 fireplaces in the 68 rooms, fourteen water-closets, an unparalleled number in those days of slop-pails and chamberpots. The carpets, upholstery, rugs, curtains and even the tablecloths were of tartan and the tartan walls were hung with the labours of Landseer. There were paintings of stags, statutes of stags, stuffed heads of stags. The heavy furniture was of African ash and dominating the hall a chill marble statue of Himself in Highland dress.

Within a mile of this stag-infested folly is the distillery built in 1825 by a wily old smuggler called John Robertson of Crathie.

At the time of Barnard's visit to *Lochnagar*, the proprietor was Henry Farquharson Begg of Tillyfour. Like most Highland distilleries, *Lochnagar* had its own farm. Here was grown the bere and barley which would be malted, fermented and distilled into whisky and here too a hundred head of cattle were fed on the draff and spent wash, thus completing a satisfactory and natural cycle.

There was no steam-power; the distillery was worked entirely by water-wheels, water coming from a reservoir filled by a spring rising on the slopes of Lochnagar which, as it descended, burgeoned into a burn gathering the waters of numerous smaller streams in its progress over heather and peatmosses.

Barnard and his friends were taken round the granaries in which the barley was stored ready for its conversion into malt. The malting-house itself was an ancient building with a stone floor and at one end was a stone steep in which thirty quarters of barley could be soaked to take up the appropriate amount of moisture to promote germination. On the floor lay the barley slowly sprouting in the semi-darkness into green malt. Close by was a kiln in which the malted barley would later be dried

Barley awaiting malting at *Benriach*, Longmorn, Elgin. In the 1890's when *Benriach* was built only first class Scottish barley would have been used, much of it grown in the fertile Laigh of Moray. Today distillation has far exceeded the annual indigenous harvests and much of the grain comes from East Anglia, various European countries and as far away as Australia. *Benriach* is one of the few remaining distilleries which still makes malt in the traditional way; the others are *Laphroaig*, *Balvenie*, *Highland Park*, *Bowmore*, *Glendronach* and *Ardbeg*.

Wet barley being turned with the broad wooden shovel or shiel on the *Benriach* malting floor. The malt has to be turned every day to prevent the roots from becoming entangled and to control the speed of germination. The barley lies on the malting floor from seven to fourteen days while the starches in the endosperm are converted into sugars to provide energy for the developing shoot. When the barley has been sufficiently modified the 'piece' is thinned to a depth of just a few inches to slow down the process. The next stage is to remove the malt to the kiln for drying.

Malt kiln at *Benriach*. Above the fire is a
perforated floor through which both
heat and peat smoke rise to dry the malt
and impart the desired flavour.

over a fire of peat cut on the neighbouring moors.

They were shown the crushers which produced the grist from the malt and the mash-house where the malt was diluted with water ready for fermenting into wash in the tun-room with its five wash backs and its timber wash charger able to hold 2,000 gallons.

In the still-house were two old pot stills, the wash still where the first stage of distillation occurred and the spirit still from which the whisky would be condensed in the worm tub cooled by a constant stream of water from the Craignagall reservoir. At the end of the still house were the low wines and feints charger, the spirit receivers and alongside the distillery were the duty-free warehouses where the spirit was left to age in oak. Here the party tasted 'some remarkably fine old whisky and thus refreshed completed our tour of inspection. We then visited the Distillery and Excise offices, the latter a rustic edifice, standing in the beautiful garden attached to Mr Begg's house. From thence we proceeded to the Brewer's neat little residence and afterwards inspected the cottages occupied by the employees of whom there were twenty.'

Barnard's tour mirrored a royal progression round *Lochnagar* forty years earlier. On September 11, 1848, Henry Farquharson Begg's father, John Begg, who had bought the distillery in 1845, sat down and wrote a note to the Queen's private secretary, intimating that the distillery was in full operation, presumably after the summer silent season, and he would be happy to vouchsafe H.R.H. Prince Albert a conducted tour round the works. The note was handed in at the Castle at nine o'clock in the evening and on the following day, while in his house next door to the distillery, Begg observed the Monarch and her Consort approaching. He opened the door and rushed out.

'We have come', said the Prince in his guttural English, 'to see through your works, Mr Begg.' 'We' included the royal couple, the Prince of Wales, the Princess Royal, Prince Alfred and Lady Cumming. As soon as they entered the distillery the two young princes rushed off to hide among the casks.

An imperious, 'Where are you young children going?' from her Majesty brought them to heel and Begg clapped one in each of his huge hands and held firmly onto them during the rest of the visit. John Begg's account of the visit reveals that Prince Albert was, in his way, as agile a conversationalist as the present consort. The royal family having been shown the whole process from the malting of the bere down to the emergence of the crystal-clear spirit, Albert looked at the locks on the safe and with lightning intuition said, 'I see you have got your locks there.' Quick as a flash Begg replied, 'These are the Queen's locks.' Her Majesty gave a hearty laugh.

When the tour was finished and they arrived once more at the door of the distillery, Begg proffered his guests a dram. 'We had cleared some that day from Bond, which I thought was very fine. H.R.H.

The Wee Geordie still at *Glen Grant*. Four of these old stills are coal-fired and they are distinguished by possessing the last water-wheel driven rummagers in Scotland. The six new stills are gas-fired. Rummagers were a device invented in the eighteenth century to prevent the wash from sticking to the bottom and sides of the still and scorching. A constantly revolving chain mesh scoured the inside of the still and kept the wash on the move. The problem was eliminated when steam coil heating was introduced.

having agreed to this, I called for a bottle and glasses (which had previously been in readiness) and presenting one glass to her Majesty, she tasted it. So also did his Royal Highness the Prince. I then presented a glass to the Princess Royal and to the Prince of Wales and Prince Alfred, all of whom tasted the spirit. H.R.H. the Prince of Wales was going to carry his glass quickly to his mouth. I checked him, saying it was very strong, and so he did not take but a very small drop of it. Afterwards the Royal Party took their departure, I thanking them for the honour of the visit they had been so generous to pay the distillery.'

Shortly after the visit, John Begg was given a Royal Warrant and appointed Distiller to the Queen. From then on, copious supplies found their way into Balmoral Castle and the lion's share disappeared down the throat of the egregious gillie, John Brown, so admired by Queen Victoria. Begg's *Royal Lochnagar*, according to the researches of Tyler Whittle in *Victoria and Albert at Home*, laid many a royal servant low. Gladstone on one occasion noted the Queen herself lacing a glass of claret with a stiff shot of *Lochnagar* and it was drunk with enthusiasm on every picnic. 'Drink', observes Mr Whittle, 'being so easy to lay hands on, and John Begg, the distiller of Easter Balmoral providing such a quantity of his special blend in bottles with an attractive blue and black label, or, more generally, by the gallon in casks, tippling was almost an occupational hazard in the royal service.'

The Queen drank her *Lochnagar* in three styles – neat, in tea or diluted with Apollinaris water. Brown just drank it. Indeed on one occasion he was so fou at Balmoral that he fell flat on his face in the royal presence. Anyone of lesser dignity and imagination than Victoria would have affected not to notice. But here was a woman who could rise to every occasion. Regarding the prone retainer with compassion, the Queen announced to the assembled court that she had distinctly felt a small earth tremor herself!

6 A Century of Change

Opposite The trough area at Chivas' Keith Bond No.2. Here up to 30 single malts, all a minimum of 12 years old, are 'dumped' into troughs for vatting. After vatting the malts will be married with grain whisky in Paisley. Chivas vat about 3½ million proof gallons of whisky here every year – that's 9 million litres of alcohol. It is an operation closely supervised by the Excise men.

Lochnagar continued to be drunk at Balmoral for the rest of the reign, but it was not made available to the commonalty until 1974, when it was for the first time bottled as a twelve-year-old single malt. Until that time it had only been procurable as part of a very expensive blended whisky called *John Begg* of which *J. B. Gold Cap* was the peak of excellence.

By the time of Queen Victoria's Diamond Jubilee in 1897, the drinking of malt whisky had fallen into decline and the preferred taste was for blended whisky – Scotch and a splash of Seltzer. The later years of the nineteenth century saw a huge boom both in production and consumption, but it was 'grain' whisky that really put Scotland on the world whisky map. The art of blending a selection of malts with grains to produce nationally advertised brands of Scotch had a revolutionary effect on the whisky trade. Over the years it turned what had been a fragmented and highly individual industry into one dominated by a few large companies. As the taste for whisky grew, the number of distilleries rose to 161. The story is a dramatic one.

Making malt whisky in a pot still is an expensive process. Because the pot still produces a spirit which is heavy with impurities, it has to be aged in oak casks for up to fifteen years before oxidation smooths its rough edges and matures it to a satisfactory mellowness. The search for labour-saving devices is not solely a twentieth-century preoccupation. Towards the end of the eighteenth century, innovators were trying to perfect a technique which would enable them to produce alcohol more cheaply. The most impressive advance was achieved by Robert Stein who built a continuous still at Kirkliston near Edinburgh in 1827. The Stein still could make whisky out of rice, barley, wheat, maize – any cereal for that matter. It was inexpensive to operate, did not require great resources of water and could therefore be set up in the centre of a town close to supplies of cheap imported grain and, more important, close to the customers. No longer would it be necessary to haul whisky on horseback from remote Highland glens.

Stein's patent still, heated by steam not by a fire, was improved when a more sophisticated version was developed by Aeneas Coffey, Inspector General of the Excise in Ireland. The two whiskies, malt and grain, existed side by side for many decades. The grain distilleries at *Port*

Dundas in Glasgow, *Carsebridge* and *Cambus* in Alloa, *Cameronbridge* in Fife, *Glenochil* at Menstrie and *Kirkliston* in West Lothian were effortlessly efficient and the malt distillers watched helplessly as this 'silent' spirit was passed off as fine old matured Scotch whisky.

For some years it had been common practice to mix various malt whiskies together to overcome the variations in quality and flavour; this 'vatting' of malts was by the 1860s replacing the marketing of single malts. By this time too, the production of grain whisky had outstripped malt. The rise of industrial prosperity in the Lowlands and the emergence of the Clyde as the greatest shipbuilding centre in the world created a new demand for whisky. Simultaneously, the disastrous onward march of phylloxera in Europe reached the vineyards of Armagnac and Cognac and the brandy-drinkers of England were forced to seek a substitute.

It was just at this time that a wine and spirit merchant called Andrew Usher, who had been experimenting for some years with whiskies produced from the blending of malt and grain, sprang into action. He found that the more aggressive and harsher malts could be tamed by the 'silent' spirit and a blend produced more to the English taste. These blander whiskies were quickly imitated by men with names like Haig, Dewar, Buchanan and Walker. 'Scotch' had arrived.

Today a blended whisky – and 95 per cent of all the whisky drunk in Britain is blended – may consist of as little as ten per cent of malt whisky or as much as fifty per cent. The *de luxe* whiskies contain high proportions of the top-quality whiskies judiciously vatted and blended; cheap, cut-price whiskies use the second- and third-class malts in small quantities drowned by grain whisky.

With the emergence of branded whiskies, their promoters began to look around and acquire malt distilleries to secure their lines of supply. Gradually the distinctions began to blur. Firms emerged which owned grain and malt distilleries and blending plants. Successful distilleries swallowed smaller ones and brand leaders began to dominate the market. None was more dominant than the Distillers' Company whose principal subsidiaries include such famous whisky names as Dailuaine-Talisker Distilleries, John Begg Ltd, Scottish Malt Distillers, Scottish Grain Distillers, James Buchanan & Co., John Dewar & Sons, John Haig & Co., D. & J. McCallum, John Walker & Sons and White Horse Distillers. Their empire includes companies involved in ancillary activities like copper-smithing, grain and seed merchandising, yeast production, malting and cooperage. With fifty distilleries at their command, D.C.L. seldom if ever buy either grain or malt whisky outside their own organisation and their blends, which account for half the export market of Scotch, are internationally known.

None of the other whisky combines comes near to matching in size or turnover the D.C.L. colossus. Today it would be unlikely that any

Opposite   The new still room at *Macallan*, Craigellachie. The distillery was built in 1824 and over the years has been greatly enlarged. Capacity was extended from six stills to twelve in 1965; to 18 in 1974 and to 21 in 1974. There are seven wash stills and fourteen spirit stills. Like many another distillery *Macallan* grew out of a farm and despite its increase in size it still produces one of the finest of the Speyside malts. The stills, once coal-fired, are now heated by gas and they need to be cleaned once a week. In the old days when coal-firing caused a heavy burning of solids the inside of the stills had to be scrubbed with a brush and sand and the man who did that entered the still through the man-door. This wash still is cleaned with caustic soda and there is seldom a need for anyone to clamber claustrophobically inside.

enterprising individual setting up a distillery would make a go of it. He would need to come under the protective umbrella of a powerful company to survive. The number of completely independent malt distilleries in Scotland can be numbered on the fingers of one hand and they have to watch their cash flow closely.

Building a distillery is a long-term gamble. The last great building boom was in the 1890s when now famous malts like *Strathmill, Ardmore, Balvenie, Glen Moray, Longmorn, Dufftown, Tamdhu, Caperdonich, Knockando* and *Speyburn* came on stream. Then the bubble burst: there was too much whisky and too few throats to pour it down. Companies collapsed, in many distilleries the fires were doused for ever and caution entered the boardrooms. In the 1960s and early 1970s, expansion was once again in the air; takeover bids and mergers made the headlines and foreign countries began investing in whisky. Japan bought shares in many distilleries and Canadian companies became even more involved in Scotland than they were before the war. Seagram, itself a part of the great Distillers' Corporation of Canada, now owns nine distilleries, some old, some newly built: *Allt a Bhainne, Benriach, Caperdonich, Glen Grant, The Glenlivet, Glen Keith, Longmorn, Strathisla* and *Braes of Glenlivet.* Hiram Walker of Canada own *Balblair, Inverleven, Loch Lomond, Glenburgie, Glencadam, Glencraig, Miltonduff, Pulteney* and *Scapa.*

If you take over an established distillery whose malt has a good reputation you have few worries. When Seagram acquired *Glenlivet*, they bought 150 years of history and the malt with the highest reputation in the world. But when they decided to build two new distilleries it was, even in these automated days, something of a gamble.

Build a lemonade plant and you've got lemonade from day one. But you have to wait three years before you can market your first drop of whisky and until it has matured for another eight or ten years you will not know whether you have created something outstanding or just a run of the still malt. Sad to say, few of the eleven malt distilleries built since the Second World War have succeeded in producing what the blenders would regard as a first-class malt.

There is an unofficial grading of malts, not dissimilar to the Médoc classification of 1855, which is accepted by most of the trade. Individual blenders have their own particular loyalties, but by and large there is not much disagreement about the ten top malts. The appraising of malts is, however, a very subjective affair; what may appeal to the nose and the palate may not necessarily be the perfect constituent of a blend. So I was very interested to see the results of a blind tasting organised by the *Sunday Times* in April, 1981. The team included two distinguished distillers and Professor Robert McDowall, author of *The Whiskies of Scotland.* They chose a *Macallan* distilled in 1963 as the outright winner. The runner-up was a ten-year old *Tormore* and this

Strathisla, Keith. Originally named *Milton*, the distillery was founded in 1786, the year that Robert Burns published his *Poems Chiefly in the Scottish Dialect.* Cooling water comes from the nearby river Isla and the water used in making the whisky is piped from the Broomhill spring above the distillery. Much of the distilled malt whisky goes into the luxury blend known as Chivas Regal. *Lagavulin* and *Bowmore* on Islay were in operation before *Strathisla* but it is without doubt the oldest working distillery on the mainland and something of a cherished show place.

Bonded warehouses at *Glenfarclas*. With the growth of centralised maltings most of the kilns once used for drying and peating the green malt have fallen into disuse. They were distinguished by their pagoda-shaped ventilators devised by an Elgin architect in the late Victorian period. This one, ignominously grounded, will never smell the peat-reek again.

Auchroisk, Mulben, Banffshire. Of all the distilleries built this century *Auchroisk* which came on stream in 1974 is the most striking and elegant. Visits from people giving 48 hours notice by telephone, particularly those interested in architecture and the conservation of the environment, can usually be arranged but the management tends to become a bit hard-pressed in the summer.

product of a post-war distillery was described as being 'well-balanced, very elegant, slightly sharp, appealing'. Third came a twelve-year-old *Glen Elgin* and the great *Glenlivet* only managed to achieve fifth place. Two of my favourite malts, *Talisker* and *Glenfarclas* received very low ratings, which proves to me at least that in the country of the blind tasting all men are blind.

That *Tormore* should score so highly certainly restores one's faith in modern technology. The distillery lies near the village of Advie on a tributary of the river Spey, seven miles north-east of Grantown. The architect was Sir Albert Richardson, veteran of the Manchester Opera House and President of the Royal Academy. By the Achvochkie Burn which flows down from Loch-an-Oir, the handsome granite-coined and white-harled building began to rise in the late 1950s. It was officially opened by the Countess of Seafield in 1960 and it sits comfortably in the forested countryside. There is, alas, however good its malt, something a little bogus about *Tormore*. Its mock watermill and its gold-faced clock set beneath a copper-sheathed cupola are the ultimate in Scottish kitsch. Every hour on the hour it chimes 'Highland Laddie' and at other carefully regulated times breaks into 'Coming through the Rye' or 'Green Grows the Barley-O'.

Braes of Glenlivet, Allt a Bhainne and *Auchroisk,* all products of the 1970s, are less whimsical. *Auchroisk,* which came on stream in 1974, is one of the most successful and exciting buildings in post-war Scotland. Even the warehouses have been blended aesthetically with the rolling moors of Mulben, four miles west of Keith. Well worth a diversion if only to see what can be achieved by a good architect and a responsible client, in this case I.D.V.

Auchroisk (pronounced 'Och-hrusk'), Gaelic for 'ford of the red stream', was built on a ninety-hectare farm which possessed a convenient spring called Dorie's Well. Its warehouses can hold fifteen million gallons of whisky, but it lies innocuously on the land and when its trees have grown it will look more pleasant than ever. Already it has won international architectural awards and one from the Angling Foundation for not incommoding the passing salmon. The temperature of its eight stills is electronically controlled.

Where *Auchroisk* hugs the ground sleekly like a neat geometrical model, *Allt a Bhainne* – Gaelic for 'burn of milk' – is reminiscent of a Tupperware arrangement: six solid boxes with variously shaped slate lids. Looked at from one angle, it has overtones of Corgarff, its starkness almost fortress-like. More than a million gallons of whisky a year can be made here. During the day, one man controls the whisky-making process; at night there are two, more for sociability than necessity.

I came across the gorse moors to *Allt a Bhainne* one summer day with cloud just brushing the rounded summit of Ben Rinnes from where the

Tormore, Advie. Equally great care was taken when Long John Distillers built *Tormore* in 1958–60. The architect was Sir Albert Richardson. A more traditional building than *Auchroisk* but no expense was spared in the detail.

Allt a Bhainne, near Dufftown, Banff-shire. Built in 1975 the raw spirit distilled here is sent by tanker for ageing at Chivas Bros. warehousing complex at Mulben. The three houses are for the manager, the brewer and the engineer.

These warehouses at Mulben lie on a 200-acre site. There are now 32 of them each holding 3½ million litres of alcohol in oak casks. Computerised, patrolled by guard dogs, a small fortune of whisky lies maturing in these giant hangars.

Bonded warehouses *Macallan* distillery, Craigellachie.

Glen Grant, Rothes. The man-door is padlocked on this still, all part of the elaborate supervision maintained by the Customs & Excise staff in their zealous determination that not a drop of excisable whisky escapes untaxed.

distillery draws its spring water. It is a bleak place with little conventional beauty. A few hundred yards from the distillery are the staff houses; in nearby fields a few cattle graze. It is easy to imagine the white hand of winter here. Inside the distillery there is the gentle hum of electrical activity; a spanner is dropped and the sound echoes round the still-house. The lorries come with malted barley and take away the casks of whisky to the Chivas Regal bonded warehouses at Keith and Malcolmburn Farm at Mulben. It is an unlikely place in which to site a £2½ million plant. Why is it not in some more easily accessible place?

A convenient moment to ponder on the importance of water. As we've seen, apart from the activating influence of yeast, malt whisky is made solely from barley and water – water in great quantity and of the softest quality. Huge amounts of water were needed in the old days to cool the condensers and many distilleries were driven by water-power. Today that's not quite so important; water for cooling the condensers can be stored and recycled, but the water used to make the mash from which the whisky will be extracted is as vital now as it was in the days of illicit distilling.

The water of the Spey valley, springs filtering out of the red granite hillsides through peat and moss beds, seems to be the ideal. Finding a clear and continuous supply of suitable water is the first preoccupation of anyone who is contemplating the siting of a distillery, and once found, the supply is guarded with obsessive attention. Barley can be procured from anywhere at any time, but if the springs run dry then the distillery must be shut down.

The traditional distilling year ran from October to May. During the summer when the burns were low the men would go out onto the moors to cut a year's supply of peat, overhaul stills and attend to the annual repair and maintenance jobs. It was always more difficult to control the growth of the green malt in hot weather and that was one more reason to suspend operations. There were other factors which made summer distilling marginal. Useful by-products of distilling are the grain husks and draff which were collected by local farmers as cattle feed. In summer when the cattle were grazing up in the lush summer shielings, the draff just went to waste, for this was in the days before techniques were developed to dry it and manufacture it into cattle pellets. Robert Munro and Richard Wilson of Keith, in a fascinating handbook on *Strathisla* distillery, recall the days when the draff used to be collected by horse and cart. 'The draff was put into sacks – about 30 bushels in all – and delivered round the town to the various cattle owners. There were about 100 cows in Keith, each owner having about two or three. Draff cost 3d per bushel plus 1d for delivery. The old farmer, a lad of 15 at the time, was paid 9d per horse, cart and man which made his earnings about seven shillings a week. He worked a ten-hour day seven days a week.'

Because distillers didn't want to waste their draff, and for a variety of other convenient reasons, distilling reached its peak in the winter months. The tradition has been retained to some extent, so that if you are travelling the roads in July and August you are likely to find the majority of distilleries idle. There have always been notable exceptions. *Benrinnes* distillery, planted on the eastern side of the mountain at a height of 1,030 feet, was always able to work through the summer, its favourable elevation allowing the malt to sprout happily.

There is not a distillery whose site was not determined principally by the water supply. *Glen Grant* was sited in 1840 by the side of the Glen Grant burn which not only provided the water needed for mashing, but all the motive power to drive the distillery machinery. Similarly *Glenrothes* was built in 1878 by the Burn of Rothes which collected its waters from the Mannoch hills; again there was such an energetic abundance that all the machinery was driven by the swirling brown water. At *Aberlour-Glenlivet* the grinding, mashing, elevating, steering and pumping machinery was driven by the waters of the Lour which sprang from the eastern shoulder of Ben Rinnes. *Dailuaine* was built on the banks of the Carron Burn, a stream fed by three rivulets all emerging from the benificent bosom of Ben Rinnes. *Cragganmore*, facing the river Spey, takes its water from the Craggan burn. *Glenfarclas* uses Ben Rinnes spring waters and *Benrinnes* distillery itself, as Barnard noted, was built where it is 'on account of the water, which rises from springs on the summit of the mountain, and can be seen on a clear day some miles distant sparkling over the prominent rocks on its downward course, passing over mossy banks and gravels which perfectly filters it before it reaches the distillery'. *Balmenach*, built on the site of several illicit operations, took its water from the Cromdale and Smugglers' burns. *Mortlach* water comes from the Conval Hills and the famous Priest Well and so it goes.

The most recent distilleries to be built were similarly positioned. When Seagram's decided to increase their production in the 1970s, they thought first of Glenlivet – after all there's no more famous centre of distilling. But where was the water to come from? I am reliably informed that old maps were consulted, geological surveys scrutinised, folklore heeded and water analysed. Experts tramped the hills searching for the ideal site. Springs were analysed for quality and their flow tested for quantity. The choice fell on the waters of the Preenie Well. A lease of land was obtained from the Balmoral Estate and the designing of the new distillery, to be called *Braes of Glenlivet*, was set in motion. Historically the Braes of Glenlivet was the least lawful part of the Highlands, because it was the least easy of access. At one time about 800 people lived in the glen, now there are fewer than a hundred. To the south are the Ladder Hills and the heights of Carn Mor and Cairn Liath. To the north-east, the River Livet and the bulk of Carn an

Opposite   Braes of Glenlivet near Tomintoul. Built 1973–4, the distillery originally had three stills; two more were added in 1975 and a sixth in 1978. Then process operator controls the whole operation from a central area mashing 400 bushels of malt every six hours. The worts are then pumped to one of the 15 washbacks where fermentation lasting two or three days takes place. From here the wash goes first to the wash still and finally to the spirit still. Four million litres of alcohol are produced in a good year and the whisky, when aged, has a typical Glenlivet aroma.

Glenlivet burn. The heartland of illicit distilling in the eighteenth century. Apart from Glencoe this is the most renowned glen in Scotland and certainly the most widely known internationally. The Livet Water flows north from the Ladder Hills to join the river Avon. The uplands remain unprentrated by roads and they are accessible only to those who are prepared to walk. At one time the glen was full of sheep and cattle.

t-Suidhe. There is a road into the Braes but when that ends you must take to your feet. So secluded was the Braes that for a long time a clandestine Roman Catholic seminary operated at Scalan House, just one mile south of the new distillery.

In the sixteenth century, the Earls of Huntly and Erroll adhered to the old faith. A memorable battle was fought in the Braes on October 3, 1594, when 1,500 ill-equipped Catholics routed a government army of 8,000 commanded by the eighteen-year-old Earl of Argyll. It is a little-known and strange by-path of Scottish history. The ninth Earl of Erroll was converted to Catholicism by a kinsman, the Jesuit Peter Hay of Delgatie. He joined with the Earls of Angus and Huntly in a conspiracy in which King Philip of Spain, still peeved by the failure of the Armada, was to land a small army on the north-east coast of Scotland and force James VI to embrace Catholicism and overthrow Elizabeth of England. Their plans were discovered and despite the success of their fight at Braes of Glenlivet, the Earls' Rebellion was crushed, Huntly castle was destroyed and James VI marched north and personally supervised the blowing up of the Earl of Erroll's sea-poised castle of Slains. So Braes of Glenlivet has certainly had its moments.

Catholicism lingered in small and remote pockets in Strathglass, Braemar, Enzie and Glenlivet. After the failure of the 1715 Jacobite rising, a small Catholic nucleus was set up about a mile from where the *Braes of Glenlivet* distillery stands at Scalan. In the old farmhouse two priests were ordained. The seminary was destroyed in 1746 by the Duke of Cumberland's troops after the failure of Culloden and the ignominious flight back to France of Bonnie Prince Charlie. The Catholic Emancipation Act of 1829 removed the necessity for the covert observance of the ancient faith. The days of the 'heather priests' were over. A school, a church and a house were built at Chapeltown of Glenlivet by the remarkable Abbé Paul Macpherson who was born at Scalan croft in 1756, became a priest in 1793 and died in Rome, a nonagenarian and Rector of the Scots College.

Walking through the old house of Scalan, which was last occupied over forty years ago, it is difficult to visualise these rooms filled with men consumed by clandestine religious zeal. Even more difficult to visualise the distilling and smuggling that went on up and down the glen at the same time. The military were stationed at Achnascraw and Demickmore and divided their time between hunting recusants and smugglers. The Slochd Burn above Scalan still contains a number of ruins which almost certainly housed illicit stills. They stand amid the summer shielings, the seasonal grazings which so took the imagination of Thomas Milne, the surveyor employed by the Duke of Gordon. 'I never saw', he reported in the 1770s, 'a country better adapted for breeding up young cattle owing to the shelter the wynding banks of Livet afford which are covered with wood and natural grass.'

The old college of Scalan in Braes of Glenlivet. The college was founded in 1717 by Bishop James Gordon, the Vicar Apostolic of Scotland, as a seminary for the education of priests. During the 80 years of its existence almost a hundred priests received part or the whole of their training within its walls. The house was repeatedly looted and laid waste by troops and it was sacked and burnt to the ground by Cumberland's redcoats after Culloden. The priests and students always returned so that during the eighteenth century Scalan represented the regenerative hub of Catholicism. The college was transferred to the site we know today from the left bank of the Crombie in 1767. When the seminary was removed in 1977 to Aquhorties in Aberdeenshire the north wing was converted into a public chapel for the people of the Braes.

Shepherd laundering a sheep, Glenlivet
burn.

The *Glenlivet* distillery where the most famous whisky in the world is made. With its visitor centre, dark grains plant, eight gas-fired stills and acres of warehousing, George Smith would be hard put to recognise the small operation he legalised at nearby Drumin in 1824. The distillery was removed to its present site at Minmore in 1858.

In May and early June, once the crops had been planted, the cattle were driven up to the summer pastures and there butter and cheese would be made and courting and merry-making would occur. Scalan perhaps takes its name from *sgalan* the Gaelic name for the crude huts or bothies built on the shielings. At one time the entire area of the Braes was used as summer grazings. 'In time,' wrote the late Dr Victor Gaffney, historian of Glenlivet, 'bothies became rectangular, seldom more than twenty feet in length and up to nine or ten wide. Whisky bothies were constructed in the same way and generally in a colony of such bothies, there was a temporary "whisky house" where a lead from the burn could be taken in.' To distinguish these days among the hardly perceptible remains of the bothies those which gave shelter to innocent dairymaids and those which housed illicit distillers is no longer possible.

Whisky played a great part in the history of the Braes and when on July 7 1973, Edgar Bronfman of the house of Seagram cut the first sod on the eleven-acre *Braes of Glenlivet* site he was following in some well-worn footsteps. The building itself, local sandstone, harled white walls, blue slated roofs, houses three stills, each with a distinctive bulge in the neck known as the 'Milton Ball' – for that particular shape is associated with Scotland's oldest working distillery of *Milton* in Keith. If you have seen *Braes of Glenlivet*, you will remember that the still-house has a bogus pagoda roof which gives the impression that barley is being malted on the site. It is a harmless enough conceit and perhaps forgiveable in a distillery so heavily automated that one man can perform the whole mystery of mashing, fermenting and double-distilling without moving from his electric console. At distilleries like *Allt a Bhainne* and *Braes of Glenlivet*, the whisky story has come full cycle. Two centuries ago a man would go happily into the Braes with a sack of barley over his shoulder and come down in the fullness of time with a keg of whisky on his back. And now today one man can once again control the whole process.

In Victorian times, with plenty of cheap labour available, whisky-making became departmentalised. Some worked the malting floors, some were in the mash-room and the tun-room; there were those operating the wash stills, others firing and coaxing the spirit stills, yet more engaged in cooperage. It was a labour-intensive co-operative endeavour.

At *Glenlivet*, for instance, in Victorian times, the pay-roll totalled fifty, some of the men admittedly working on the attached farm with its 120 head of cattle which consumed the surplus draff and spent wash. Those fifty men produced between them 20,000 gallons of pure Highland malt every year; a mere 4,000 gallons per worker. At *Braes of Glenlivet*, 400 bushels of malt are mashed every six hours. From the fifteen wash backs the worts pass to the two wash stills and thence to the

Edradour, near Pitlochry.
Manager, Jenneth Maclean.

Only small amounts of malt are distilled
in this the smallest and most traditional
distillery in Scotland.

four spirit stills. Nine men producing a million gallons of whisky –
111,000 gallons per worker per year!

If big is economically beautiful, small still exists. At one time, the
smallest distillery in the United Kingdom was to be found at Grandtully
on the river Tay, a village said to be the model for Tullyvolan in Sir
Walter Scott's novel *Waverley*. It was, noted Barnard, 'the most primitive work we have ever seen. The whole "bag of tricks" could be put
inside a barn and a child four years old could jump across the streamlet
which drives the water-wheel and does all the work of the Distillery.'
Grandtully was worked by the owner, Donald Thomson, and a work-
man and between them they produced 5,000 gallons a year.

Grandtully has long since ceased operations and pride of place in the
Small-is-Beautiful stakes has fallen to the miniature distillery of
Edradour, just to the south of Pitlochry. On my way to see *Edradour*, I
stayed the night on the banks of the Tay at Dunkeld in the retreat the
Duke of Atholl built for himself and his Duchess in 1900. The Duchess
had the house cunningly constructed with a system of double corridors
so arranged that her eye never fell directly on the classes – servitors
with coal scuttles, lassies with feather dusters and red-cheeked
tweenies. Dunkeld House is now a hotel; set in over a hundred acres, it
is surrounded by noble trees. As one sits in the dining room, contemplating the breakfast menu of Arbroath smokies, poached Finnan haddock, poached kippers, chilled melon, green figs, porridge and cream,
devilled kidneys, grilled steak and sauté potatoes, mixed grill, Ayrshire
bacon, and eggs cooked in several ways, one's eye falls on bowling and
putting greens and the tea-brown Tay of which the hotel owns one and
a half salmon-rich miles.

A good place from which to start a whisky trail. But not in July. We
went first to look round Bell's imposing ivy-hung distillery of Blair
Athol, with its unique tiled roof, at the south end of Pitlochry town, and
although we were given a warm welcome the stills were cold, the mash
tuns empty, it was holiday time. Built in 1826 and watered by the
springs of Ben Vrackie which flow into the Kinnaird Burn, *Blair Athol*
was founded by a Conachar who was the descendant of the Conachar
celebrated in verse by Sir Walter Scott in *The Fair Maid of Perth*.

We were told we'd have no trouble in finding *Edradour*. 'Half a mile
down the main road and then a sharp turn by the school.' We overshot
it and made a second attempt. It was a very sharp turn up so minor a
road that you felt it could hardly be leading to an enterprise which had
that May won the Queen's Award for Export Achievement. The road
wound up the hill past high hedges, fields, smallholdings and trim
villas until eventually we came upon the whitewashed stone walls and
the blue slate roofs of *Edradour*, perched alongside a cascading burn.
Kenneth Maclean, the manager, was working in the still-house when
we crossed the wooden bridge over the stream. 'You're in luck,' he said,

'the exciseman is here so you can see the warehouses.' So small is the operation that there is neither room nor need for a resident exciseman – when he is required he comes up from Perth to put his key alongside Mr Maclean's so that the doll's-house doors into surely the smallest bonded warehouse in Scotland can be opened. You bend almost double to get in, your head brushes the low-hung rafters. The distillery buildings date back to 1837 and the whole operation is housed in an area no larger than a modern bungalow. Right up to the end of the Second World War, the distillery was worked by water-power, an eccentric survival from the old days. Electricity was installed in 1947, but a lot of the old machinery is still serviceable.

The company which owns *Edradour* prides itself on its hand-made image, but consider the output too small to market it as a single malt. It can be found in the excellent *de luxe* blended whisky King's Ransom, and they also bottle it, vatted with one other Highland malt, under the name of *Glenforres-Glenlivet*, despite the fact that there is no such place as Glenforres and *Edradour* itself is nearly fifty miles away from Glenlivet.

If you venture into the Highlands, you may be confused by the prevalence of the name 'Glenlivet'. At one time there were 28 distilleries using 'Glenlivet' as a prestigious appendage. Today there are still sixteen distilleries in places as far removed from Glenlivet as Rothes, Forres, Aberlour, Keith, Dufftown and Strathspey with a magic dash of Glenlivet to their name. There are parallels. The eighteen-and-a-half-acre Côte d'Or vineyard of Montrachet, which produces the most celebrated dry white wine of France, has several neighbours who have latched -Montrachet onto their own names. I'm told there are 28 French wines with La Tour in their name, all hoping no doubt to be mistaken for the great Château Latour. And it's the same with Glenlivet.

There is, however, only one distillery entitled to call itself *Glenlivet* and that is the successor to the original distillery established in the glen by George Smith in 1824. In 1825 and 1826, three more legal distilleries were set up in Glenlivet, but the smuggling mafia forced them out of business. In the mid-nineteenth century, Captain William Grant of Ruthven, who commanded a small military force which had been brought in to lend support to the excise officers and who had married George Smith's daughter Margaret, decided to start distilling at Auchorachan, another spot in the glen. He was so conscious of the value of the name 'Glenlivet' in association with whisky that he arranged to have an advertisement inserted in the *North British Advertiser*, warning its readers to be wary of imitations: *'Captain William Grant* of the Auchorachan Distillery *Glenlivet* begs to acquaint Connoisseurs in whiskey, that in that far-flung Glen, which wholly belongs to the Duke of Richmond, there is no other Distillery than *his own* and that of

On the banks of the Livet.

George Smith of the Drumin Glenlivet Distillery – nor within several miles of it and the Public is respectfully cautioned against any other Distillery assuming that title.'

Auchorachan distillery was closed in 1850 on the death of Captain Grant, and George Smith's distillery resumed its role as sole whisky monarch of the glen. But more and more distilleries began climbing on the Glenlivet bandwagon. On November 6, 1865, the Duke of Richmond and Gordon wrote a letter in the hope that it might give his loyal tenant some protection against those who were taking the name of his glen in vain: *'The District of Glenlivet, a part of the Gordon property in Scotland belongs to me. My tenants George and John Gordon Smith, whose distillery of malt whiskey is called "The Glenlivet Distillery" – are the only distillers in the district – Richmond.'*

Even that didn't work. The number of distilleries which had added the glamour of Glenlivet to their name had reached two figures. John Gordon Smith, who had inherited the *Glenlivet* distillery in 1871, went to court to stake his legal claim. The court decided that the whisky produced at Minmore, whither the distillery had been moved in 1858 from its original site at Upper Drumin, was the only one entitled to call itself *'The Glenlivet'*. It was decreed that the others continue to attach 'Glenlivet' to their distilleries only if they qualified it with a hyphen.

If 'Glenlivet' has such a cachet, does that mean that geography plays a significant part in the final taste and flavour of a malt whisky? When it was customary for whisky to be matured in the distillery of its origin, it was generally believed that ageing the spirit in the vicinity of the stills was the right and proper thing to do – if you made whisky in Islay you should mature it in Islay.

There have always been those who claim to detect in the whisky of that seashore distillery, *Laphroaig* a strong odour of seaweed and ozone. The high moisture content of the air in the islands was thought to benefit maturing whisky. The cold, crisp winters of Speyside, the marine humidity of Orkney, the softer climate of the Lowlands have all been cited as having a noticeable influence on the end product. Such is the poetic imagination of the Celt that I have even been told that casks placed on earth-floored warehouses matured more gratifyingly than those resting on stone or planks. It is true that casks lose less from evaporation in a damp environment than they would in a dry one; it is true too that a warehouse high in humidity diminishes the strength of the whisky, whereas a dry place has only a mild effect over the years on the alcoholic strength of the spirit.

Many illusions have been debunked in the post-war years. It is now the custom for blenders who have ordered raw malt whisky from distilleries to remove it immediately from its place of birth to centralised warehouses in the Lowlands. Here, in enormous hangars as large as football pitches, the hogsheads and butts are stacked to the roof. It is

The standing stone of Achorachan.

Achorachan is a hamlet on the banks of the Livet six miles south of Ballindalloch. The story is told that about 70 or 80 years ago the standing stone was dug out of the ground and used as a door lintel for a farm building. From the time the stone was put into the building the family who had perpetrated this insensitive act had nothing but ill luck. Eventually the old lady of the house told the sons that their luck wouldn't return until the stone was put back in the field. But she was not heeded. Disaster piled on disaster until the lads pulled the stone out of the wall and carted it back to where it had come from. Their luck immediately changed for the better.

an economical and rational way of doing things, but ugly in the extreme. The companies involved in constructing these big bonded warehouses surrounded by chain-link fencing have been made to erect tree belts round them, but they remain depressingly obtrusive.

If temperature and humidity are no longer considered to be that vital in the maturing of whisky, what other myths are left? Wood is certainly a major influence. All whisky is aged in porous and permeable oak casks and a prolonged exposure to wood and air makes profound changes in the flavour and taste of the whisky. The oldest whisky I have tasted was a *Macallan* which had been forty years in cask and had become so smooth and subtle that, if put to the test, I could not have differentiated it from a great cognac. In his *Scotch Whisky*, my friend David Daiches records drinking an enjoyable 68-year-old malt from the *Longmorn* distillery at Elgin.

The oldest recorded whisky ever drunk was consumed by Joseph Mitchell in the house of Macdonald of Borrodale on the shores of Loch-nan-Uamh. Macdonald's grandfather had sheltered Prince Charles on the first and last nights he spent in Scotland in his quest for the crown. Old Macdonald and all his followers went out with the chief of Clan Ranald to join the Prince in 1745, but before leaving they buried all their plate and valuables and a quantity of whisky in a neighbouring moss. Most of the men who had hidden the family's possessions died at Culloden. Although the plate was soon discovered, the whisky was not. It was not until 1810 that a keg of whisky was laid bare during the spring peat-cutting. It had been buried in the moss for sixty or seventy years and when Mitchell was offered some at Borrodale House in 1838 it was well over ninety years old. It was, said Mitchell, an 'insinuating whisky (which) excited in us the most benevolent feelings during the whole evening'.

At a much later period than this, it was found that old sherry casks were ideal for ageing whisky. Not only did they impart a pleasant smoothness, but they also coloured the spirit so that it looked like a fino or an amontillado. A few merchants try to use sherry casks for their fillings whenever they can. At *Macallan*, for instance, they believe so strongly in the effect that sherry casks can have that they still mature all their output in casks made in Jerez – an extravagance which they feel is completely justified.

Whatever the influences – barley, malting, peating, mashing, distilling, maturing – there is no doubt that malt whiskies are highly individual and, to those who have spent a lifetime in the industry, immediately recognisable. Some are full-bodied, some sweet, others might be described as peaty, dry, delicate, fruity, sharp, light, nutty, woody, aromatic . . . Compared with the whisky of smuggling days, they are light and smooth, but they retain an unmistakable character which has never been imitated anywhere else in the world.

7 Dufftown Stands on Seven Stills

Opposite Balvenie castle which has given its name to the nearby distillery owned by Wm. Grant & Sons. Balvenie was one of the earliest stone castles to be built in Scotland. Its original courtyard plan dates from the thirteenth century but it was greatly altered in the sixteenth century by the Stewart Earls of Atholl who demolished the south east front and built a three-storey Renaissance tower-house known as the Atholl Building. It has been roofless since 1742.

If you were looking for the centre of whisky land, the choice might well fall on Dufftown. 'Rome', it has been said, 'stands on seven hills; Dufftown stands on seven stills.' Although the surrounding hills are rich in historic associations, the whisky capital itself is a modern creation, laid out in 1817 at the behest of James Duff, the fourth Earl of Fife, to relieve unemployment after the Napoleonic wars. Duff chose the site for his little town well. It stands at the confluence of the Fiddich and the Dullan whose waters are, local distillers will tell you, every bit as good as those of the nearby Livet.

Within easy walking distance of the 1839 Clock Tower are two castles, a church dating from the twelfth century and seven distilleries: *Mortlach* (1823), *Convalmore* (1869), *Glenfiddich* (1866), *Balvenie* (1892), *Dufftown* (1896), *Glendullan* (1897) and *Pittyvaich* which came on stream in 1974.

Golfing enthusiasts may well want to play the nine holes of Britain's highest course which lies a mile south on the road to Tomintoul; historians should not miss Balvenie castle which lies opposite *Glenfiddich*. One of the earliest stone castles in Scotland, it acquired what remains of its present shape during the tenure of the Earls of Atholl in the sixteenth century, but lost its roof in 1724.

If you walk up Glen Fiddich on the road to Rhynie, you will come to Upper Keithack and the castle of Auchindown, which is believed to have been erected in the eleventh century as a stronghold against the Danes. Surrounded by prehistoric earthworks and standing above Glen Fiddich, its ruins are visible for miles around. It was burnt down in the sixteenth century by The Mackintosh, and it stands now as a romantic stone prelude to the Cabrach, that unique and once whisky-infested plateau.

Just south of the town is the thirteenth-century parish church of Mortlach, built on the remains of a cell established by St Moluag. Malcolm II is said to have defeated the Vikings on the site of the church in the year 1006 and the interior is rich in medieval stonework.

Glenfiddich, whose malt is on sale all over the world, is efficiently geared to the annual descent of tourists and the original distillery has been converted to a hospitable visitor centre. The distillery was built by

Knockando church. The village is dominated by distant Ben Rinnes from whose
springs several local distilleries derive
their water.

Disused station built to serve *Dailuaine* on the old Strathspey line opened in 1863. Many distilleries in the Spey valley had their own private railway sidings and the Great North's line from Keith to Boat of Garten with the branch to Elgin through Rothes proved a boon to the distilleries along its route. By the time the Beeching cuts truncated the railway system in the Highlands most distilleries had begun to use lorries and road tankers but the lines which remain still carry a proportion of whisky traffic.

The Knockando station once served *Tamdhu*. It is now a visitor centre for the distillery where the Saladin maltings can be seen at work.

a Major Grant whose descendants still control the firm. So successful was he that in 1892 he bought the lands of Balvenie and built a second distillery. *Balvenie* and *Glenfiddich* share the same water supply from the Robbie Dubh spring and use the same malt, but they produce two dissimilar whiskies, proof that man may propose but whisky disposes itself. *Glenfiddich* has 27 pot stills, some heated by coal and some by gas, and half of all the malt whisky exported from Scotland in bottle is distilled here. Small wonder that some 40,000 visitors a year come to see it being made.

Mortlach, sited in the Dell of Dullan, is fed by waters from the Conval Hills and the famous Priest Well. *Convalmore*, on the outskirts of Duff-town, has four stills and a dark grain plant which converts the waste products of the distillery into cattle food. *Dufftown*, built near Morlach church, takes its water from Jock's Well and on the neighbouring farmland Arthur Bell recently built *Pittyvaich* whose stills are an exact replica of those at *Dufftown*. *Glendullan* was the last of the Dufftown distilleries to be built in the nineteenth century; it was rebuilt in 1962 and enlarged by the addition of a second distillery in 1972.

If you're a good walker, you could stretch on to *Allt a Bhainne* (see page 158) which is four miles to the south of the town on the slopes of Ben Rinnes. If you are less energetic you could take a hundred-mile drive round the very heart of the region. Leave Dufftown on the B9009 for Tomintoul and you'll be following the Dullan Water through Glen Rinnes, passing the 2,755-foot summit of Ben Rinnes on the right-hand side, devoid of smugglers now, but rich in heady memories. On to Glenlivet and its famous distillery, and then south along the River Livet to Tomnavoulin and the new distillery of *Tamnavulin-Glenlivet* which lies in the hills on the west bank of the Livet. It is architecturally hardly exciting, but looks purposeful enough to produce in excess of a million gallons of light-bodied Speyside malt a year.

Glenfiddich is the only distillery on Speyside to bottle its own malt whisky on site.

Two miles down the road is the 1898 distillery of *Knockando*, the first to be custom built with the newfangled electric light. It produces a medium-bodied, slightly nutty malt. The name itself, *Cnoc-an-dhu*, means the black hillock.

Close by are the distilleries of *Cardow* and *Tamdhu* which has its own Saladin malting (see Chapter X). The water for *Cardow* (pronounced 'Car-dew') is brought from the Mannoch hills. The distillery was extensively modernised in the early 1960s and the still-house, mash-house and tun-room were rebuilt. But it is an historic site and one sanctified by illicit distilling. *Tamdhu* has skilfully converted its old railway station into a reception area. The distillery was sited there to take advantage of the Strathspey line, but during the economies of the sixties the lines were removed and *Tamdhu*, like many another distillery, was forced to rely on the road for contact with the outside world.

Knockando is noted too for its woollen mill whose machinery dates

The weaving mill at Knockando was built
in th year 1800. It is probably the oldest
working mill in the country and the
machinery, much repaired, is still turning out high grade tweed which is
exported to various parts of the world.

Kildrummy castle. This is reputed to be the finest example of thirteenth century courtyard castle in Scotland. Dr W. Douglas Simpson, the foremost authority on Kildrummy, wrote: 'in every detail of its architecture and masonry it is a masterpiece of the highest merit; as a ruin it is grandly picturesque and truly described as "the noblest of Northern castles".'

It was modelled on Chateau de Coucy near Laon and work began in the reign of Alexander II. Its role was to guard the route to Moray and its six great towers, its splendid hall and chapel with three tall lancet windows was one of the wonders of the north. The gardens are largely an Edwardian legacy, the work of Colonel James Ogston who built a replica of the 'Auld Brig o' Balgownie' which lies on the northern outskirts of Aberdeen. A team of Japanese were imported to construct the Water Garden which runs through the Back Den and in 1903 the rock formations were created for the alpine garden at the foot of the quarry face. The skilful mix of trees, shrubs and flowers forms a perfect setting for the ruins.

Craigievar castle. Completed in 1626 the castle has a vaulted Great Hall and is one of the most outstanding castle homes in Europe. It remains virtually unaltered and in perfect condition.

Glenbuchat castle. The castle was built in 1590 by John Gordon. It has long been a ruin; the Gordon estates were forefeited after the abortive uprising of 1745 and bought by the Duffs who built Glenbuchat Lodge at the head of the glen.

Glamis castle. The castle where Queen Elizabeth the Queen mother spent much of her childhood, dates mainly from the last quarter of the seventeenth century. There was a much earlier building on the site dating from the eleventh century. The paintings, tapestries and furniture are particularly fine.

The butterfly-haunted Italian Garden,
Glamis.

back to the nineteenth century; some of it, operated now by a Londoner, is the oldest working machinery of its kind in the country. You can see the whole process from the carding of the raw wool to the weaving of the tweed – an exciting working museum which is proving to be highly profitable.

The road crosses the moors now and rises to Tomintoul, lying on a sandstone ridge between the glen of Avon and the vale of the Water of Conglass. When the Duke of Gordon built it, he called it Tamantoul and it was dismissed by Queen Victoria who noted in her diary on September 5, 1860, 'Tomintoul is the most tumble-down, poor-looking place I ever saw – a long street with three inns, miserable dirty-looking houses and people, and a sad look of wretchedness about it. Grant told me it was the dirtiest, poorest village in the whole of the Highlands.' *Tomintoul*, built in 1965, is higher than any other distillery. As Victorian guide books used to say, it 'need not detain the traveller'.

From Tomintoul you could take the Lecht Road over the Ladder Hills down to Cock Bridge, Balmoral and Ballater and return north to Dufftown by Kildrummy Castle and the superb ruined medieval church of Auchindoir.

There are almost as many castles in the north-east as there are distilleries. Kildrummy itself is one of the noblest ruins in Scotland, the only Scottish relic of a thirteenth-century courtyard castle in existence. Modelled on the Château de Coucy near Laon in northern France, it was raised to protect the route north over the Mounth to Strathbogie and the lowlands of the Moray Firth.

In the great age of castle-building during the late eleventh and twelfth centuries, the north-east was an unruly territory. Saxon chiefs fleeing from the Normans, and Normans themselves acquisitive for land, staked out their claims and threw up stockades to protect themselves and their retainers. The lord lived in the keep, the household in the bailey.

Dunottar commanded the route north to Aberdeen; Edzell and Brechin were sited strategically in Strathmore, the Norman motte of Strathbogie rises above the gorge of the Deveron. Towards the end of the Middle Ages, the castles gave place to fortified towers and noble houses. Keeps were converted into defensible mansions and gradually gave place to imposing piles like Glamis and Crathes, constructed more for domestic convenience than a state of siege. They retained the castellation of earlier days, but no arrows were fired in anger from their battlements, no boiling oil dropped from their towers.

Some ancient monuments were sacked by rival clans, others were set on fire, yet more left to crumble when the owners decided to abandon them in favour of something smaller and cosier. The castles and fortified houses of the north-east, dating from Norman times, culminated in crenellated Victorian replicas of Balmoral which were com-

Brown Caterthun hill fort, Angus, 5½ miles north west of Brechin. The white and brown Caterthuns lie a mile apart. The name 'Caithir Dun' means fort of worship. The remains of the Brown Fort are turf with concentric circles of ramp and ditch.

Stone circle at Colmeallie farm, Glen Esk. Two concentric rings with a central hollow. Only seven stones remain upstanding – a mini-Callernish well worth a detour.

The Manse Stone, Glamis. An almost
perfect example, in the garden of the
manse at Glamis, of an eighth or ninth-
century Pictish cross-slab and symbol-
stone. Ten feet high, it has a decorative
cross on the south side and fish and ser-
pent symbols on the reverse side.

Aberlemno Stone. Aberlemno, which
lies midway between Forfar and
Brechin, is famed for its superb group of
Pictish symbol-stones. The carvings are
some 1200 years old.

missioned by wealthy industrialists as summer-houses and shooting lodges. Whether or not they thought the outraged tenants might one day rise as a protest against so ostentatious a display of wealth and privilege I don't know, but there's many an arrow-slit window in these preposterous piles through which, as a last resort, a beer baron might fire upon the revolting peasantry with his hand-chased, double-barrelled, breech-loading ·450 Purdey.

Sprinkled with castles, mansions, fertile farmland and the finest herds of cattle in Britain, this must surely be a promised land. When I first visited the hinterland of Aberdeenshire, I was overwhelmed by the corporeal presence of the past, the profusion of Pictish stones. Were all these ancient and legendary monuments to be planted in Essex, what excitement they would create. Imagine the Londoner being able to take a day trip to the castles of Glenbuchat, Drum, Tilquhillie Midmar, Craigievar, Balfluig. Apart from nearly twenty castles in the Dee and Donside, there are a further dozen monumental castles in Kincardine, all within an hour's drive of Aberdeen.

I spent a few days just driving round the coastline. I took the road north from Aberdeen up the A975 to Newburgh, which lies on the estuary of a burn that teems with fish unique for their size – the Ythan trout are world famous and the obsessive fisherman may well hole up in the Udny Arms and stay for a week out of sheer delight. If he does, he'll be in the heart of the incredible Sands of Forvie on whose bone-white dunes you could film *Beau Geste* and get away with it.

These 1,700 acres surrounding the estuary of the Ythan (once a tributary of the Rhine) are now an open-air laboratory for zoologists from Aberdeen University. At the height of the breeding season there are more than 3,000 eider ducks and drakes here, big clamorous birds you can hear from far away. The Ythan is a summer larder for the terns on their 10,000-mile migratory flight to the Antarctic. What makes Forvie so important to the researchers is its remarkable status as the only estuary of such ornithological significance left in an unpolluted state. Upstream there are no factories voiding their effluent.

Inland there lies the valley of the Garioch, once known as the Granary of Aberdeenshire, a sheltered vale bounded by hills. In the market town of Old Meldrum is the *Glengarioch* distillery, founded in 1797, which has established for itself a unique reputation. The cycle of distillation produces excessive amounts of hot water which usually go to waste. At *Tomatin* they have experimented with the rearing of young elvers into eels, at *Glenfarclas* there have been pioneering attempts to breed crayfish using warm water from the distillery and high-protein whisky by-products as fishfood. *Glangarioch* (pronounce it 'Glen-geery') is growing cyclamens, tomatoes, cucumbers and salads as a year-round spin-off from the production of whisky. It's an interesting departure; the whisky produced by a distillery usually makes little impact on the local community. It provides employment and no more. It is frequently matured, blended and consumed miles from its point of origin. But if, from the distillery, can come forth fruit and vegetables and fish, what a healthy bonus that will be!

I stayed the night at Collieston on the coast where the ill-fated Gillespie made some of his most lucrative smuggling hauls. In its prime, Collieston was packed with fishing boats; in the 1880s, nearly seventy boats fished out of its picturesque Cornish-looking harbour. Today Collieston speldings are only a folk memory. T. E. Lawrence stayed here and thought speldings a bit overrated, 'tasting like dull veal'.

As we walk round the harbour, a cool mist begins to drift in from the sea; here it's called a *har*. I see what Lawrence meant when he wrote, 'the concealed sun makes all things half-luminous so that the gulls become silvered whenever they dip suddenly to turn a knife-edge cartwheel in the spray.' I wonder if, when he walked on the northern sands of Forvie, he was reminded of the ambivalent footprints he had left in other, warmer sands.

Drive north round the coast and you pass the modest installation where North Sea oil is brought ashore at Cruden Bay. The pipeline enters a small complex before setting off on its arcane journey inland – a piece of technology which buries a bonanza discreetly beneath the farmtouns of Aberdeen.

A mile farther on, we park the car where the sign says 'Bullars of Buchan'. Dr Johnson, on his journey to the Hebrides, came here and was rowed 'stout and wonderfully alert' to see this vertiginous chasm in the cliffs. In May the grass is ablaze with wild flowers, seathrift hangs on the cliff edges and the keening of birds drowns the dredge of the surf 200 feet below. There are gulls by the thousand, guillemots, fulmars, puffins, kittiwakes – the cliff edges are picketed with nesting birds, limed with guano. Tread warily in this birdman's paradise, the path round the cliffs is narrow, the downward view dizzy. Bullars in my book ranks with Handa and Fair Isle for its breathtaking grandstand view of seabirds in their natural state.

It's only a few miles on to Peterhead, the bustling Buchan, sometime herring port with its red granite harbour and boatyards. At first sight it's a stern town; on the way you pass the barbed-wire perimeter of the maximum security jail – it's difficult to imagine that in the eighteenth century Peterhead was a watering place and spa. In the mid-nineteenth century, it sent more ships to the Greenland and Davis Straits in pursuit of whales than any other town in Britain. In 1820, fifteen whaling ships returned with over a hundred Atlantic whales, and when the whaling declined herring took its place. The herring have gone too, but whisky remains. In 1875, a distillery was built on the seashore to the south of Peterhead and named *Glenugie*. It is the most easterly distillery in

Glengarioch, Old Meldrum. One of the oldest distilleries in Scotland with one of the most progressive attitudes to conserving energy. The greenhouses are warmed by waste heat and grow both plants and vegetables. Here a consignment of *Glengarioch* tomatoes are being packed for the market. Maybe an enterprising local barman could invent a rival for the Bloody Mary – why not a Bloody Meldrum, tomato juice and *Glengarioch* on the rocks?

Scotland and its whisky is used solely for blending by its owners, Long John International.

Take the road north from Peterhead to Fraserburgh and on to the small, cliff-hugging fishing ports of Pennan, Crovie and the steeply precipitous village of Gardenstown. The little port lies at the foot of the red cliffs of the Bay of Gamrie, not the sort of place you'd be advised to drop into towing a caravan. It is a dour, north-east Portofino with terrain so abrupt that some of the three-storied houses have cliff-side access to each floor. They say that Gardenstown is one of the richest fishing villages in Scotland, although these days most of the boats operate out of Macduff, five miles west along the coast. When I arrive I find six boats on the slips, in various stages of building or repair. Boat-building is very much a family business on this north-east coast. The waterfront is given over to the shops of fish salesmen and ships' chandlers.

In 1960, Macduff acquired a distillery and since the nearby Glendeveron supplies its water, the malt bottled at five years old and 75 proof is known as *Glendeveron*. Macduff has the best harbour on the coast and in neighbouring Banff one of the most splendid examples of eighteenth-century architecture in Scotland – Duff House, modelled by William Adam on the Villa Borghese. *Banff* distillery established in 1824 was removed to a new site in 1863.

More interesting than *Banff* is *Glenglassaugh*, two miles inland from the picturesque fishing village of Portsoy, famous for its serpentine marble, some of it purchased in the eighteenth century by Louis XIV to furnish mantelpieces for the Palace of Versailles. When Alfred Barnard came to Portsoy in the 1880s, he admired the plains, 'laden with most luxuriant crops which delighted our eyes and gladdened our hearts; farmhouses were scattered here and there, surrounded by ample barns and stabling, all betokening the easy circumstances of the farmers, and on our right the beautiful sea stretched out as far as the eye could reach'.

Barnard had noted in his monumental expedition round Scotland that all the distilleries he and his friends visited were sited either on the sea-shore or on the side of a mountain, and on asking why he was told: 'We must have plenty of water power and good water so we select the banks of a quickly flowing stream. Then again we use home-grown barley and only peat of the finest quality for drying the malt; also we believe that a good climate and pure air are indispensable in the production of a delicate spirit like Whisky.'

Glenglassaugh, built in 1875, took its water from the Glassaugh river which rises in the Knock Hills and its malt from a farm of eighty acres which grew some of the finest barley in the district. It was modernised in 1964 and bears little relation to the rural distillery Barnard saw on his travels.

Opposite Crovie, an old village on the north east coast of Aberdeen, less than a mile from Gardenstown. A Gamrie schoolmaster writing in the 1860's described Crovie as having one gable end to the sea, the other boreknto the cliffs 'like a brood of young seafowl, nestling with their heads under their dam'. Before the Great Storm of January 1953 Crovie was a marginally thriving fishing village, but the storm persuaded some of the families to migrate to Gardenstown and many of the houses are now holiday homes.

Beyond Portsoy lies Cullen, noted village of the skink, that delicious smoked haddock soup, and Buckie with its *Inchgower* distillery. Built in 1871, it eventually passed into the hands of Buckie Town Council from whom it was bought in 1936 for £3,000 by Arthur Bell and Sons.

From Buckie it is but a short drive to Elgin, the market town of the fertile Laigh of Moray, long famous for its superior barley and the large number of distilleries which surround it – noted names all of them: *Linkwood, Benriach, Glen Moray, Miltonduff, Longmorn, Glen Elgin, Glenlossie, Mannochmore, Coleburn.*

This is the headquarters of Scottish Malt Distillers, the subsidiary of D.C.L., which began life in 1914 as a company running five Lowland distilleries and now controls almost half the malt distilleries in Scotland. Other whisky companies too have their headquarters in this old, bustling town on the Lossie. Its elegant stone mansions in the High Street and its superb thirteenth-century cathedral are some measure of its role as royal burgh and focal point of the whole of the north-east.

Forres at the mouth of the Findhorn; that perfect specimen of Georgian town planning, Fochabers; the old and new towns of Keith; eighteenth-century Huntly, another creation of the Gordon family at the confluence of the Bogie and the Deveron; Charlestown of Aberlour on the banks of the Spey, laid out in 1812 by Charles Grant of Wester Elchies, are all in the heart of distilling country.

In Rothes, a town founded on the banks of the Spey in 1766, home now of *Caperdonich, Glen Grant, Glenrothes, Glen Spey* and *Speyburn,* you will find the echoing workshops of Grant & Sons where the whisky industry's pot stills and wash backs, the spirit safes and receivers are made. At Craigellachie is Willie Taylor's family cooperage where casks are assembled and repaired for a score of northern distilleries. Here there is a smell of whisky in the air and the famous White Horse distillery of *Craigellachie* built by Alexander Edward of Forres and Peter Mackie in 1890.

And there are the lesser 'towns', relics of the old farmtouns of the north-east which were little more than farmsteads. At the peak of their Victorian prosperity, handsome teams of Clydesdale horses worked the land and the farms, each with its grieve, bailiff, orramen, ploughmen, shepherds, dairymaids and loons, were self-contained and almost self-supporting. They are gone, but their names linger on signposts and maps: Milltown, Watertoun, Farmtown, Eastertown, Kirkton. And the old roads linger too. Jock's road across the Grampians from Glen Callater to Glen Doll and Glen Clova trod by many a smuggler in the past and hundreds of weekend hillwalkers today. There's the Whisky Road or Priest's Road, so called because the minister of Lochlee in Glen Esk also held the cure of Lethnot and was forced to commute in the service of God between his flocks. There are many well-worn tracks crossing the Grampians from Deeside to Tarfside in Glen Esk. The best

Craigellachie lies at the confluence of the Fiddich and the Spey; the chimney rises from the ninety year old distillery belonging to White Horse Distillers.

Fishing for salmon on a summer evening on the Spey. This, the second longest river in Scotland is noted both for its distilleries and its salmon; it is rivalled for catches only by the Tay and the Tweed.

Riveting hoops
at the Speyside
Cooperage,
Craigellachie.

Checking the staves.

Willie Taylor's cooperage at Craigel-lachie employs 23 men who make and repair casks for almost all the Speyside distilleries. Sound, well-made and well-maintained oak casks are essential for the maturing of whisky whether it is grain or malt. No spirit can be legally called whisky unless it has been aged for a minimum of three years in wood.

Raising a barrel is highly skilled work; fitting the thirty or so staves together calls for a good eye and an educated hand. In the old days when all the sherry imported into Britain came in casks whisky was matured in sherry oak; now almost all Scotch whisky is aged in American oak casks remade from barrels previously used for maturing bourbon. The casks are broken down in the U.S. and shipped across in bundles. It takes one and a quarter of these bundles or shooks to make a dump hogshead which will hold between 54 and 56 gallons of whisky. The raw materials – the wood and the handmade iron hoops – cost about £30. The price of a remade barrel in 1982 was £40. A good cooper can raise and finish five hogsheads in a day. It has been found that although malt whisky matures well in these remade American oak casks they do not continue imparting the desired qualities to the malt indefinitely. Just as the first growth châteaux of Bordeaux specify new *barriques* for each vintage so distilleries proud of the quality of their malt are most careful in their choice of casks.

Top right   Raising a cask.

Bottom right   Casks awaiting repair.

Glen Doll is a western extension of Glen
Clova and is noted for its alpine flora,
rare plants and ferns. The famous track
known as Jock's Road rises from the
White Water of Glen Doll on its high
level route to Braemar.

known in whisky annals is the Fungle across the hills from Aboyne. Even older is the road linking Banchory and Fettercairn, passing over Cairn o'Mount, a pass used long before the smugglers by such notable personages as Macbeth, Edward I and Montrose. There were wolves on these hills until the eighteenth century, and many a bloody confrontation between excisemen and smugglers in the nineteenth.

The famous Cabrach, metalled now, was once a mainline whisky route from Strath Spey to Donside and the track across the Ladder Hills from Donside to Glenlivet jingled with the harness of the whisky ponies. Traces of old illicit bothies can be made out faintly in the hills even to this day if you have enough imagination, and if your imagination is lacking you can repair to the Glen Esk Folk Museum in the Birks of Ardoch where you'll be shown ample evidence of past illicitry.

8 The Wind Howled, The Snow Drifted Higher

Opposite General Wade's famous Lecht road to Tomintoul.

By the end of September, the distilleries have resumed production and the tourists have gone home. The seasonal hotels shut their doors and it begins to get dark earlier and earlier in the afternoon. The annual slaughter on the grouse moors is over, the stag heads have been airfreighted in triumph back to Stuttgart or Buenos Aires, the salmon have swum downstream on their urgent, involuntary migration to feeding grounds somewhere in the North Atlantic or the Arctic Ocean. The high plateaux harbour mountain hare, snow bunting, wildcats and golden eagles and, reaching higher every year, urban man in pursuit of leisure.

'Winter Ski-ing Weekends in Aviemore': the flyposters are stuck all over London. Take the night train from Euston and by nine o'clock on Saturday morning you're out on the nursery slopes. Coaches and cars home in on Aviemore from all over Britain and the demand for more and more ski runs in places like the Cairngorms and Glenshee seems insatiable.

It is now possible, thanks to commercial enterprise, for any one to stroll to the summit of Cairngorm in plimsolls. Leaving the fish and chips and the toffee papers of Aviemore behind you, take the road to Coylumbridge, press on past pine-fringed Loch Morlich and on through Glenmore Forest Park until you emerge at the chairlift which will sweep you up to the Ptarmigan restaurant. From there it's a short stretch up to the 4,084-foot summit, an arctic relic covered with tundra vegetation.

The Cairngorms are the highest mountain massif in Britain; formidably vast, formidably bleak. During the Second World War, commandoes were trained here and veterans of Everest among them reckoned the blizzards were more severe here than anything they had faced in the Himalayas. The Nature Conservancy Council is seriously concerned about the threat to their national nature reserve on the Cairngorm summit plateau, particularly in view of the chairlift company's application for outline planning consent to extend their tows westward into Coire an-t-Sneachda, Coire an Lochain and Lurchers Gully. Already the regional council have approved a road and car park to provide access to three large snowfields.

The Nature Conservancy Council claim that montane heaths, mires and grasslands would be damaged, if not permanently impaired, by building operations and with the improved summer access, birds like the golden plover, the dotterel and the ptarmigan could be threatened. The Cairngorms are a Grade 1 site of international significance and the argument of the Council is a simple one: destroy this and you destroy something irreplaceably unique.

The Countryside Commission is concerned too, and as I write, the battlelines are being drawn up. This is a wilderness area which looks impregnable, but the hand of man is everywhere. If you own an estate in the Highlands, you can do almost anything you like with it. A householder in Glasgow or Edinburgh has to apply for planning permission if he wishes to put a shed up in his back garden. If a land owner wishes to bulldoze a ten-mile Land-Rover track across his acres so that wealthy but unfit sportsmen can be driven up to the grouse they have paid to shoot, no one can prevent him. Conservationists regard these ill-made scars across the moors as another potential threat to the geomorphological features of the uplands.

Fortunately, there are still huge tracts of land which deter all but the most determined. Look east from the summit of Cairngorm, for instance, and there isn't a sign of human habitation until the tiny hamlet of Milton of Whitehouse, 28 miles to the east. Staggering off on your own in these parts is not to be recommended in winter and those who have only seen the whisky roads in high summer would be chilled by the thought of the Lecht in January or February.

North of Corgarff, at a height of 1,344 feet, lies Cock Bridge and the stretch of road which rises to over 2,100 feet connecting Strathdon with Strathavon. This is one of the highest and wildest passes in Scotland and from September onwards there is always the risk of snow. The road, narrow and twisting, is the only direct route between Aberdeen and the Central Highlands. When it is blocked by winter blizzards all traffic has to make an eighty-mile detour through the Cabrach to reach Tomintoul. As I write these words in March, Radio Scotland is warning motorists that three major routes are blocked – Braemar to Perth, Cock Bridge to Tomintoul and Rhynie to Dufftown – and news is coming in of a mountain rescue in blizzard conditions in Glen Doll. Weather for the fireside, not the hills. Even when illicit distilling flourished here in the early nineteenth century, there couldn't have been much going on in the winter. With the wind in the north, clear blue skies can fill with snowclouds in minutes, the thermometer falls alarmingly and Strathdon begins to look like a bad day in the Yukon. The local G.P. dons snow-shoes and in some years winter persists until June.

There are many stories told of travellers who perished in sudden snowstorms and the graveyard at Corgarff is sprinkled with stones erected to those who fatally lost their way. Perhaps the most touching story concerns a young girl immortalised as the Lassie of the Lecht, who set out a hundred years ago to make her way to the house where she was in service. It wasn't until the following spring that her body was found. Alongside her tombstone, a simple slate marks the grave of an unknown traveller who perished in the great blizzard of 1937.

Nine miles up the road, twenty-foot snow-drifts are not uncommon and farming is a polar experience. People who live round here keep three weeks' supply of food in the house, for although the A939 can be kept open by snow-ploughs, if you live a couple of miles off the main road you either have to stay indoors or get your skis out.

Until a few years ago, the Lecht road was blocked almost continuously throughout the winter and yet flying across the high hills you could see a whole unused world with a remarkable leisure potential. Enthusiasts had been battling their way to the uplands behind the snow-ploughs to grab the odd bit of weekend ski-ing, but the priority to keep the Lecht road open was low. In the late 1970s, a group of businessmen formed the Lecht Ski Company. Lifts were imported from Grenoble and although Upper Strathdon is not going to become another St Moritz, it could give the whole run-down area a welcome shot in the arm and the conservationists further cause for alarm.

Further south, the Glenshee Chairlift Company has plans to expand and royal Braemar might well find itself as busy in the winter-time as it is in summer. Perhaps the one deterrent is the dearth of sunshine, but already at Glenshee the slopes are crowded beyond capacity and early risers drive up for a day on skis from as far away as Dundee, Edinburgh and Glasgow.

Now and again, even with the most modern snow-ploughs, huge areas of the Highlands come to a winter standstill, blocked by impenetrable drifts. I doubt if Queen Victoria would have conceived such a passion for Don and Deeside if she could have seen it in the grip of a severe winter. In the early idyllic summer years at Balmoral, the Queen delighted in adventuring forth into her kingdom incognito. She fancied herself in the role of ordinary traveller in much the same way as Marie Antoinette liked to play at being a milkmaid in the Hameau at Versailles.

On Friday September 20, 1861, just after seven in the evening, she and Albert and their small but conspicuous entourage arrived at the village of Fettercairn. 'It was very small – not a creature stirring and we got out at a quiet little inn, the "Ramsay Arms", quite unobserved and went at once upstairs. There was a very nice drawing room and next to it a dining-room, both very clean and tidy – then to the left our bed-room which was excessively small, but also very clean and neat. We dined at eight, a very nice, clean, good dinner.' All was discreet and decorous. 'The landlord and landlady knew who we were, but *no one else* and they kept the secret admirably.' On the following day, a Satur-

day, the royal party in their procession of carriages passed Fasque, the country house of Sir Thomas Gladstone: 'The harvest and everything seemed prosperous and the country was very pretty.'

One hundred and twenty years later, Fasque still stands and is still owned by the Gladstones; the Ramsay Arms is still an inn, lit by electricity now, not candlelight, but still serving 'nice, clean, good dinners'. I know, because on a bitterly cold winter's day recently I visited both Fasque and Fettercairn and experienced for the first time the full force of a white-out in north-east Scotland.

Fettercairn lies to the south of the historic pass of Cairn o'Mount which links it with Banchory and Deeside; every winter the link is broken when the road which reaches an altitude of nearly 1,500 feet becomes snowed up and impassable. The Howe of the Mearns is an area rich in historic houses. There's Fettercairn House itself, built in Restoration days by John, first Earl of Middleton, Lord High Commissioner to the Scottish Parliament. A mile to the south-west is Balbegno castle, which dates from 1569, and there are the ruins of Edzell castle, once visited by Mary Queen of Scots. But Fasque House is a lesser-known and somewhat later mansion. I had gone there to make a programme in the I.T.V. series *Treasures in Store.* The principle liquid treasure at Fasque had been removed several years earlier when the contents of its cellar were auctioned. The cellars, moist and consistent in temperature, had housed what Michael Broadbent, Christie's wine expert, had described on encountering it as the equivalent in vinous terms to the opening of Tutankhamen's tomb. There wasn't a bottle younger than 1914 and some of the treasures dated back to the mid-nineteenth century.

The origins of Fasque go back to the eighteenth century when Sir Alexander Ramsey demolished his small but elegant house and built a large and romantic replacement. Its architect was probably John Patterson, who was for many years Robert Adam's Clerk of Works. In 1829, the Ramseys sold Fasque to the son of a Leith corn merchant who owned slave plantations in the West Indies and had the money and the whim to play the laird. John Gladstone sired six children of whom much the most famous was William Ewart. The house has now been in the possession of the Gladstone family for 150 years and from the 1880s onward, bachelor Sir John Gladstone and his spinster sister Mary seem to have thrown nothing away.

Fasque is a trove of bric-a-brac and bygones, and I was lucky enough to be shown around by the present incumbent, Peter Gladstone, who remembers his childhood in the big stone house with its enormous kitchen, its sculleries, laundry rooms, larder, stables and its imposing staircase. 'It's reputed', Peter Gladstone told me, 'to be the biggest double-cantilevered staircase in the world. There's one in Washington which is almost as big but not quite, which we're very pleased about.'

Edzell lies six miles north of Brechin almost at the mouth of Glen Esk. Edzell once had the most splendid castle in Angus but it now lies in ruins. Sir David Lindsay designed a spacious garden or pleasance in 1602 whose walls are ornamented by elaborate carvings in stone. On the east wall of this unique garden are the ecclesiastical deities, on the south the sciences and on the west the theological and cardinal virtues.

The family in their heyday were fed by four acres of kitchen gardens, venison from the hills, salmon from the rivers, sheep and beef from the home farm and all manner of game. Not so long ago there were 26 servants living in at Fasque; the oldest of them, one of the last survivors, died towards the end of the 1970s. She remembered coming into the vast stone-flagged kitchen on cold mornings, climbing up onto the kitchen table using the chopping block as a stepping stone and scrubbing the table top with sand and vinegar. She was thirteen at the time and her day finished at ten in the evening.

High on the wall in the kitchen is the grim legend, 'After work play. After play work.' Scrubbing, polishing, fetching and carrying, Fasque was a never-ending conveyor belt of hard labour.

The house was so engrossing that almost before we knew it the light had begun to fade and we realised that for some time now it had been snowing. The wind too had risen. Peter Gladstone came through to the drawing room where we were filming and said that if we didn't leave at once we'd be stranded for the night. As the Gladstones were living in a small wing of the house and the rest of the rambling pile was unheated, we made a dash for the cars.

We just made it through the bonnet-high snow down the drive to the main road. There were no other cars in sight; snow was banked along the hedges. With headlights on, wipers ineffective against the whirling blizzard, we managed to slide and skid back into Fettercairn. Outside the Ramsay Arms there were several abandoned cars. Getting back to Edzell and our hotel was out of the question. The road to Aberdeen was blocked, the overhead power cables down. Undaunted, the landlord and landlady of the Ramsay Arms took the seven of us in. There were candles in the lounge and heat from a Jötul wood-burning stove. The meal, cooked on Calor gas stoves, was more than nice, clean and good, it was terrific. We had scotch broth, venison pate made from local deer meat, and trout with almonds.

Outside, the wind howled, the snow drifted higher and Aberdeen remained pleasantly cut off. I retail this story not to prove how immutable the hospitality of the Highlands is, but to draw attention to the harsh weather conditions which are very much part of life in the regions where the finest whisky is made.

By the following morning the snow-ploughs had moved in and the road was opened, but there was still no electricity and scores of hamlets and remote farmhouses were cut off and likely to remain so for days, living out of the larder.

This might be a suitable place to comment on the kind of food you may be offered when exploring the whisky roads. The news is not universally good, a disappointment in a part of Scotland noted worldwide for its beef, its salmon and its venison. Aberdeen itself was once the busiest fishing port in the world: on a good day 800 tons of fish

Opposite Fasque house, Fettercairn, home of the Gladstone family since 1829. The laundry contains a box mangle and this cast-iron laundry stove for keeping 'sad' irons hot. Sad irons were made in all sizes and shapes for ironing everything from delicate lace to heavy linen sheets. The word is thought to be derived from the Middle English 'sad' meaning to compress or make stiff.

would be laid out in the market – half a mile of cod, haddock, halibut, ling. All round the coast the fishing villages were famous for their specialities. Findon in Kincardineshire was the first village to split haddocks open and smoke them and create the delicious golden finnan haddie. In the smuggling village of Collieston they cleaned the haddock and whiting and dried them in the sun – Collieston speldings were famous all over the north-east. At Arbroath and Auchmithie they smoked their haddocks whole; at Cullen Bay in Banffshire they took smoked haddock and made it into a soup or *skink* with onion, mashed potato and milk. At Musselburgh they would dredge mussels from the beds at the mouth of the river Esk and prepare a brose with milk and oatmeal.

Barley broth, bannocks, Aberdeen butteries, brochan, howtowdie, collops-in-the-pan, crowdie, Forfar bridies, haggis, partan bree, Tweed kettle, pickled herring, porridge, scones, shortbread, cock-a-leekie soup, Scotch broth, venison pasties – the Scots kitchen is a creative one. There are few other cities in Britain which have produced two such distinctive inventions as marmalade and Dundee cake. There are no better grouse in the world than those shot on Scottish moors, no better raspberries than those grown in Blairgowrie.

But if you drive through the Highlands in the winter, you'll find much of it shuttered and closed. The remoter hotels are seasonal; their doors open in the late spring, close with the October gales. Many of them are former shooting lodges commanding prominent and breathtaking views over glen and moor and loch, but the food often comes out of packets and tins. Fine fresh poached salmon will be served with bottled salad cream, frozen peas, a tinned pineapple ring and a scoop of canned corn. The potatoes, in a land which has given the world the finest potatoes in the whole litany of potato-dom, are likely to have come out of a sachet in the form of tasteless granules. The milk on your porridge (from a packet) will almost certainly be U.H.T. The Scots have embraced convenience food with the enthusiasm with which they originally embraced Calvinism, and that makes eating out on the whisky trail a numbing experience. At lunch you are likely to be offered nothing more exciting than packet soup and those cotton wool toasted sandwiches which are steam-heated inside a cellophane wrapping until the bread softens to the consistency of polycell and the cheese filling spreads like bubble gum. Unenterprising hoteliers and innkeepers are encouraged in their lethargy by guests who are almost totally indifferent to the food on their plates. When any old thing will do, then any old rubbish is likely to be produced.

I think I'm right in saying that there was only one meal that Dr Johnson encountered on his journey in Scotland to the western islands that he was not able to eat. It was presented to him at the Red Lion in Elgin. The fish was good but the beef collops and mutton chops were inedible. Nowadays nothing is inedible; it is unfortunately all too often tasteless and so denatured that it slips down without leaving any noticeable impression behind.

Not a hundred miles from Elgin, I dined recently off food which had all been pre-prepared and microwaved into instant availability. The menu was full of out-of-season dishes and elaborate boil-in-the-bag *'haute cuisine'* portions prepared in a commercial kitchen hundreds of miles away. There was nothing on offer that had not done time in the freezer. Amid the alien corn on the cob, snails, imported pâté, *Sachertorte* and tutti-frutti, the broiler veal and battery chicken, there was a strong taste of monosodium glutamate and artificial flavourings, but no taste of Scotland. One longed for something simple – a bowl of broth, a herring in oatmeal, a few slices of Aberdeen Angus beef, a mutton chop.

The Scottish Tourist Board is well aware that it has some of the finest scenery in the world within its remit, and some of the worst hotel food. A few years ago the Board launched its 'Taste of Scotland' scheme to encourage caterers to specialise in the traditional good things that when well done are well worth doing – boiled gigot of lamb, braised haunch of venison, cloutie dumpling, colcannon, ham and haddie, mutton pie, stovies and game soup.

When planning an exploration of the whisky roads, it would be prudent to arm yourself with a copy of the S.T.B.'s *A Taste of Scotland* brochure which although not exhaustive has a useful list of hotels and restaurants which are offering a selection of local dishes. Wise too to arm yourself with the Consumers' Association's two invaluable handbooks for those who care about their stomach and their comfort, *The Good Food Guide* and *The Good Hotel Guide*. Using them, it is possible to make your way through the glens and not be confronted at the end of the day with a plateful of processed junk.

Opposite   Glen Shee sculpture park, Spittal of Glen Shee.

Carrbridge sculpture park. Carrbridge has an award-winning visitor centre which, if not the first in Europe, was certainly among the earliest. Open all the year round it has a restaurant, shops, an audio-visual show and wildlife films.

9   A Search for Proof Positive

The Mill of Auchindoun three miles outside Dufftown on the Huntly road. Here in Edwardian times a busy co-operative of distillers were illicitly at work. Unfortunately one of the members felt that he wasn't getting his fair share of the profits and in pique he went into Dufftown and shopped his colleagues to the Excise. When they arrived the Customs men found little evidence. However one of the family was given three months imprisonment.

The last well-documented outbreak of illicit distilling took place just over a hundred years ago when, in 1880, the Malt Tax was abolished and the Preventive Force was considerably reduced in numbers. Until 1880, the manufacture of malt could only be carried on by licensed traders. As it took up to twenty days to convert barley into malt, the period during which a smuggler was liable to detection if he did his own malting was dangerously long. Now that malt could be bought legally, the illicit distiller was only at risk during the four or five days in which he was fermenting and distilling.

A further incentive was the Crofters' Act which for the first time afforded a unique security of tenure to families who until then could be removed from their holdings for the slightest irregularity or misdemeanour. The fear of being made homeless if caught breaking the law had deterred quite a few crofters and cottars from the attractions of smuggling. And the attractions were many. When Ian Macdonald gave his celebrated lecture to the Gaelic Society of Inverness in 1887, he pointed out that barley could that year be bought for 23s a quarter. That was enough to make fourteen or sixteen gallons of whisky and it could be sold at up to £1 a gallon. 'Allowing for all contingencies, payment of carriage, liberal consumption during manufacture, and generous treatment of friends and neighbours, some £8 or £10 can be netted from an outlay of 23s.'

But the quality of illicit malt whisky no longer compared favourably with the legal distillation. While the still licence was in force between 1787 and 1814, the legal distiller sacrificed quality and flavour to quantity, which is why George IV called for smuggler's Glenlivet and not the duty-paid stuff. The prejudice in favour of illicit whisky persisted long after legally produced malt whisky had proved itself superior in every way – except for the tax it attracted.

The smuggler, as Ian Macdonald knew only too well from his experience as an exciseman, was operating under all sorts of disadvantages, including a fear of discovery, which necessarily forced him to work in a hurry and the best whisky needs a great deal of time and care in its preparation:

He begins by purchasing inferior barley which as a rule is imper-
fectly malted. He brews without more idea of proper heats than
dipping his finger or seeing his face in the water and the quantity of
water used is regulated by the size and number of his vessels. His
setting heat is decided by another dip of the finger and supposing he
has yeast of good quality, the fermentation of his worts depends on
the weather as he cannot regulate the temperature in his temporary
bothy, although he often uses sacks and blankets, and may during
the night kindle a fire. But the most fatal defect in the smuggler's
appliances is the construction of his still. Ordinary stills have head
elevations from 12 to 18 feet which serves for purposes of rectifica-
tion, as the fusel oils and other essential oils and acids fall back into
the still, while the alcoholic vapour, which is more volatile, passes
over to the worm, where it becomes condensed. The smuggler's still
has no head elevation, the still-head being as flat as an old blue
bonnet and consequently the essential oils and acids pass over with
the alcohol into the worm. These can only be eliminated by storing
the spirits some time in wood but the smuggler, as a rule, sends his
spirits out new in jars and bottles, so that the smuggled whisky, if
taken in considerable quantities is actually poisonous.

So when I set out to look for illicit whisky in the Highlands, with Ian
Macdonald's words in my mind, I wasn't all that keen to taste it. And
that was just as well for it soon became clear that moonshine was not to
be run to ground without a great deal of patience.

'That would be telling', said an old man knocking his pipe out against
the stone dyke on which we were both leaning. I had asked him, as I
had asked countless others in this whisky country, if there was any
lawless distilling going on these days.

'There's no doubt it *did* go on long after it was thought to have
ceased. But I wouldn't like to say what's going on today. You'd need to
be very quiet about it. Maybe you could set up a still away in the hills
where you'd be on your own but I've not heard of it, not these thirty
years or more.'

An exciseman in Dufftown was even less optimistic that I might
stumble on some midnight moonshiners. 'If there is any distilling these
days, it's more likely to be in the towns among immigrants who see no
reason why they shouldn't brew up a bit of something or other.'

I'd heard, I said, that in the Spey valley, there was at least one
enthusiast smuggling wash out of a distillery and completing the process in the unexcisable safety of his home. But you'd need many a
bucketful of wash to make a bottle of whisky. And as another exciseman said, 'Why bother taking wash out of a distillery, when with a little
ingenuity you can take the whisky out?'

The precautions against the unlawful leakage of whisky are elabo-

The famous sma' still of Auchindoun is
now in the possession of Willie Taylor of
Craigellachie. A few hours before the
law arrived at the mill the still had been
dismantled and the vital parts were
buried in a peat moss up in the Cabrach.
One man knew where it was hidden,
gamekeeper Alec Nicol, and many years
later he sold it to Willie for £20. As the
law required, Willie handed it over to the
Excise authorities who effectively nob-
bled it by boring the mandatory holes in
the bottom and plugging the neck of the
still with lead. Willie, a great romantic at
heart and a passionate believer along
with Burns that 'whisky and freedom
gang the gither', believes that illicitry still
flourishes in the Haughs of Cromdale, a
favourite haunt of eighteenth-century
smugglers

rate and they haven't changed for generations. From the moment that the malted barley is mashed, the resident excise officer in a distillery keeps an official eye on its progress from wash to low wines, from low wines to whisky. Everything from the distiller's safe to the bonded warehouses is under lock and key. The manager of a distillery cannot enter his own warehouses without informing the exciseman. But despite all the obstacles to enterprise, it isn't difficult, if you are single-minded enough, to take home a few samples of your work.

If all else fails and you are very thirsty, you can always bore a hole in a barrel. A long-pensioned distillery worker on Speyside told me how in the days when casks of whisky were taken by horse and cart to the nearest railway station there was no need to go thirsty.

'They used to stop in a secluded place, bore a hole in the bottom of one of the barrels and put a shovel under it. Mind you, they would have *cleaned* the shovel of course. That was raw spirit of course but most people like it raw. In fact I remember one day when I'd just started work as a lad seeing an old man a bit the worse for drink. "Oh," said one of the coopers, "he's taken a shovelful too many!" '

Help-yourself devices used by distillery workers at *Glen Grant*. The tubular 'dog' on the right was found inside a cask when it was being taken apart for repair.

Most distilleries have a collection of what they call 'dogs'. At *Glen Grant* distillery they'll show you curved brass containers just the right shape to slip under your belt and smuggle out of the gate under a buttoned-up coat. Extracting whisky from the casks in the warehouse is relatively simple. You just remove the bung and lower a 'dog' into the spirit. A Heinz tomato ketchup bottle on a string will do, or if you are a perfectionist you will have made your own more durable dog – a copper tube sealed at the bottom and fitted with a screwtop. You lower it into the cask of your choice, let it gurgle full, bring it out, screw the top on tight and with the dog dangling from your braces or belt you walk out nonchalantly at the end of your shift, trying to look as if you haven't got a stiff leg.

Perhaps someone walking out with a suspiciously rheumatic hip movement may be stopped at the gate and parted from his trusty dog; sometimes the cylinder is wedged in the cask to remain undiscovered until it is broken down for restaving in the cooperage. Spiriting away the spirit certainly goes on, but compared with the evaporation of two per cent, it is a drop in the annual multi-million gallonage of whisky produced in Scotland. If you are particularly observant towards closing time in pubs where distillery workers gather, you may well see an unlabelled half bottle of clear liquid being passed round. One of my voluntary researchers actually rang to tell me that he had been offered in Rothes a taste of what he took to be an illicit distillation – proof positive that somewhere a small surreptitious still was being worked. When we made a few inquiries, we found that the whisky, raw and unreduced in strength, had not been illicitly made – it had merely been illicitly removed from a distillery. 'Helping yourself is quite common,' a distillery manager told me, 'mind you, it sometimes gets out of hand. We had a laddie who was actually taking it out in four-gallon jerricans once. We sent him packing straightaway!'

The cottage production of *poitin*, so marked a part of life in rural Ireland, particularly the wild west of Connemara, has, it seems, no counterpart in the Highlands of Scotland. There are rumours, of course, but many of them on investigation turn out to be no more substantial than the sighting of flying saucers. Unidentified flying stills are reputed to exist in Melvaig, on Speyside, in the islands, and in the hills wherever the hopeful arm can point.

'Over there,' an old shepherd said, pointing to the great bulk of the Cairngorms, 'right up beyond the glen you'll see traces of two hundred stills.' That magic and mythical number again, akin to Ali Baba and the forty thieves, or the 1001 Arabian Nights. 'There were 200 families making whisky there to my knowledge not that long ago. And they'd take it over the hills to Brechin and Aberdeen.'

How long ago would that be?

'Two hundred stills', the old man said wistfully, relishing the thought of the peat smoke rising and the worms condensing all that free-flowing whisky in stone-brown ice-cold burns. 'I wouldn't like to give you the names, but they were well known enough in these parts. Great days they were, great days!'

But how long ago?

'Well when I was a boy I remember my father telling me you could see the fires everywhere. Everyone was at it and very good stuff it was too, better often than the finest *Glenlivet*.'

Just as there has always been a predisposition to believe in Second Sight in the Highlands, so when it comes to illegal distilling few people are prepared to deny its existence altogether. 'I'm sure it is going on,' a brewer in Dufftown told me, 'but where and when I couldn't say. If I *did* know I wouldn't tell you and if *I* knew then a lot more people would know and it wouldn't be long before the law knew too.'

In the summer of 1980, I discussed illicit distilling with a Perth exciseman. Did he think it was going on?

'Oh yes. In fact one of my colleagues was up climbing a few mountains in the north-west of Scotland not so long ago and he met this old crofter fellow. They got on the crack, having a chat, and he said, "Sitting here I can see the sites of four illicit stills." So my friend said, "I don't want you to tell me because I work for the Customs and Excise", and he said "O.K. I won't", but there we are! Apparently we still have them, but I doubt it goes on near distilleries. If you're a stillman and you cannot steal spirit, there's something wrong with you.'

But when you examine cases where people have been brought to trial, then the time scale gets a bit warped. There was the case of the man who worked at *Tomatin* who was caught in his mother-in-law's house at Carrbridge making whisky. How long ago was that? Well it was just after the last war, maybe thirty years ago or more. The last authentic case seems to have been in the early 1950s and it was chronicled by Steve Sillett in *Illicit Scotch*. It was in the wilds of Gairloch, a bothy with a corrugated iron roof excavated to a depth of three feet below ground level. The still was an ordinary household hot-water tank and all the paraphernalia of whisky-making was there. 'Fresh water was on tap, and the chimney was constructed in such a way that the smoke from the still fire diffused through the entire length of the overlying peat-stack. It was truly an ingenious construction.'

And you would have to be very ingenious to produce good whisky in such ad hoc conditions. Although many distillery workers prefer raw spirit to the aged, it would not be to the general taste. Rough, fiery, it needs the subtle education of oak, the long schooling of the cask to graduate it from immaturity to an acceptable degree of smoothness.

A friend of mine, who had spent a lifetime as an exciseman, dismissed illicit whisky as rotgut; strong and dreadful. 'A lot of people think that because it's illicit and doesn't cost more than a few pence it ought to be a great drink. All whisky has to be aged, some of it isn't really drinkable until it's twelve years old, but the stuff they make in the heather, you'd be mad to drink half of it!'

He told me that north of Ullapool you would be well on the way to finding an illicit still. 'The road comes to an end, but the croft houses go on and there's a rough track. You know that you're being watched from the minute you arrive and you'd have no chance of stumbling on anything.'

That was twenty years ago. Would they still be turning out illegal *uisge*?

'Well let me put it this way: if it's done anywhere in Scotland it's done there. You see, the snag of making it somewhere like the Spey valley is the distribution. You sell someone a bottle and they'll boast about it and then everyone will know. But up on the west coast when I was there last, they had a fairly good union, they had security and no one was talking. The head maker was at that stage an old man and there were others under him to whom he handed on the secret of distillation. I had been told about it by a local who knew me well enough to trust me even though I was working for the Excise. Oh I knew they were at it. Wherever I went, this friend of mine would, as soon as he introduced me, say quickly, "He's an exciseman", and then every tongue was on its guard.'

I asked him as a loyal officer of Her Majesty's Customs and Excise what he had done about this hotbed of smuggling?

'Nothing at all. Regretfully, I have a fellow feeling for illicit distillers. With the rate of duty as it is nowadays, I think it's a damned shame that a Scotsman can't make his own drink. No, looking back I'm afraid 'I made a very poor exciseman!'

Back in the Spey valley I made many more enquiries. I think everyone entered into the spirit of my quest, dredging up their own stories of illicitry in the glens. On some days I began to be convinced that I was about to be taken, suitably blind-folded of course, to some active bothy; on the other days I had my doubts that there was anything to be seen at all.

'I've heard', a distillery manager told me, 'of two illicit stills in the last few years operating within ten miles of Elgin. I've heard about certain tradesmen doing repairs to certain utensils. In this part of the world it's got to be going on in some croft outhouse. You see you've got plenty cold running water there, and plenty security. I mean if you and I were going to distil some illegal spirits, we wouldn't use a farmhouse down here, we'd choose something away up the hill and we'd take great pains that nobody heard about it.'

As home-distilling is looked upon more as a hobby than a villainy, quite a few people are prepared to admit to having had a smuggler in the family.

'Apparently', one distillery worker told me, 'my great-uncle and an accomplice used to acquire wash from a distillery near Keith. It came to them in milk churns and they made a bothy on Ben Rinnes. They were making it just for themselves and a few friends really. They only acquired the wash when they were down to their last two or three kegs. They did their distilling and then they used to dig a hole and bury the kegs on the slopes of Ben Rinnes. Now with the last consignment they made they were nearly caught. They had a tip-off the excisemen were coming. The hole had been dug, they bunged in the casks, filled it with earth and bracken whatever, but in the rush they forgot to mark it. And he swears, my great-uncle, that to this day there are still two or three hoggies of distillate lying in a hole somewhere on Ben Rinnes. Mind you, he was talking forty years back!'

Somehow all the tales told to me in the vibrant present tense turned out to be past history when it came to the crunch.

'Can you take me there?' I asked one contact who had described an elaborate operation occurring not a mile from where we stood. 'Take you there, of course I can take you there. I could take you there backwards in the dark. *But I'm not going to!*'

Great-uncles occur with remarkable regularity in accounts of illicit distilling, presumably on the theory that fathers are too close for comfort, grandfathers a bit too much in the distant historical past. Having sifted through all the first-hand encounters I have heard while writing this book, the one which has the most authentic note of truth came from someone who works for a London publisher. She was staying with her uncle in the Aboyne area in May 1961. This is her story:

'I used to go fishing with my uncle on the Dee and one day the gillie asked me if I'd like to go and get some bait with him. Actually it wasn't bait we went for at all. He really wanted to show me this still. I'm not clear about where it was; I'm not disguising the place because I really don't know where we wound up. It was up in the hills near a farmhouse, quite off the beaten track. We went into this shed, a sort of lean-to, and there was a copper still. What impressed me more than anything was that the whisky was colourless. I always thought whisky was brown. Oh yes I tasted it. It was very strong, rough you might say, but clear as water. I wasn't to say anything about it to my uncle the gillie said and I never did.'

Not a mile from Glenlivet, I recorded the following highly circumstantial story of contemporary moonshining. 'About eighteen months ago', said my contact, 'I was in pub near here called 'The Croft' and this guy was very drunk. Knowing that I managed a distillery, he was making rude remarks about modern whisky distillers – the stuff wasn't nearly as good as the stuff he used to make in his day and so on. It turned out that this character had been making illicit whisky in a sort of co-operative. He procured the barley possibly from his own croft, the second guy did the malting. After malting, they ground it between two stones and then the grist was transferred to the third partner who mashed and fermented it. When the fermentation was finished, he put the wash into some old-fashioned milk churns and it was then transported several miles to accomplice number three. He did the distilling and his bothy was somewhere on Ben Rinnes, the hill was over there They were never found out and they reckon the reason was that the three different departments were miles apart.'

And were they still at it?

'Oh well who knows? Anyway I met a great-uncle of mine about a year ago for the first time and I was telling him this story and he said, "Och, I mind fine who they were but I wouldn't divulge their names." '

I had a perfunctory search of Ben Rinnes. Admittedly I didn't stretch right to its 2,700-foot peak, but I came across no sign of liquid buried treasure, not even a tumble of stones that might have been a whisky bothy. But I've just had a message. By phone. 'I saw Willie last night,' a kinsman from Keith said, speaking softly in case They should be listening, 'he said if you come and see him he'd give you positive proof that illicit distilling was going on.'

Hold everything, Willie, I'm on my way . . .

10 How Whisky is Made

Malt whisky is so called because it is made solely from malted barley. The first stage is the conversion of barley into malt. Originally every distillery had its own malting floors where, after prolonged steeping in water, the moistened barley was spread out on the stone or concrete in beds about two feet in depth. As the barley began to grow and produce a root and a shoot called an acrospire, the 'piece' as it is called began to generate quite a lot of heat. The barley was turned sometimes twice a day with wooden shovels to enable air to circulate and also to prevent the rootlets growing into a soggy mass. Each time the barley was turned it was distributed more thinly over the floor, a skilful process which controlled the progress of the germination and sometimes took up to a fortnight depending on the humidity and temperature. When the rootlet was about an eighth of an inch long and the acrospire had reached about two-thirds of the length of the ear of barley, all the available starch had been converted into fermentable sugars.

Today there are very few distilleries which still use their floor maltings; the constant hand-turning of the barley has been replaced by mechanical maltings which specialise in the art and supply distilleries all over Scotland. There are two methods of converting barley into malt. In drum malting, the steeped barley is placed in huge perforated drums which revolve at a controlled speed, turning the barley which is also subjected to cooling blasts of air. The alternative system was devised by M. Charles Saladin. In Saladin maltings, the moist barley is poured into a long metal or concrete trough known as a box. As it germinates, the barley is turned by a rotating paddle.

In all three methods, the chemical changes which occur are identical. The enzymes cytase and diastase convert the starch in the barley into dextrin and then into maltose. When this stage of germination has been reached, further activity is halted by drying the green malt in a kiln.

The kiln is a square stone building with a pointed pagoda-shaped roof. Below is a fire of coke and peat; suspended above on a perforated floor is the green malt. As it dries, it is also impregnated with peat reek which gives malt whisky its characteristic flavour. The more heavily the fire is peated, the smokier the final flavour of the whisky.

When the malt is fully dried and cured, it is stored for several weeks to allow it to recover from the traumatic metamorphosis. The next job is to shake and beat the malt to eliminate the husks and the tiny hairy rootlets which sprouted during germination. After the malt has been dressed in this way, it is coarsely milled between automatic rollers. Each bushel of malt (42 lbs or 19 kilos) should yield between 2·8 and 2·9 proof gallons of whisky. A proof gallon consists of 57 per cent alcohol and 43 per cent water by volume.

The ground malt, known as grist, is stored in a hopper until it is required for mashing. In the mash tun, carefully regulated amounts of hot but not boiling water interact with the malt and extract the soluble sugars. The liquid produced is known as worts; several waters are added to ensure that all the sugars are extracted. The residue of grain husks is used as cattle food.

The wort is cooled and run into the fermenting or wash backs where specially prepared yeast is added to start the cycle of fermentation. The porridgy wort seethes and bubbles, releasing large quantities of carbon dioxide gas. Fermentation can take up to three days, depending on the weather and the water. When the process is complete, you are left with a weak, beer-like alcohol called wash.

The next step is to separate the spirit from the wash by distillation. From the wash back, the liquid is pumped to the wash charger from where it will go into the onion-shaped copper still. Stills are heated either externally by coal, oil or gas or internally by steam coils. The method of heating, the shape of the still, the speed at which the still is run, are all considered to exercise a profound, even mystical effect on the rising vapours.

Alcohol fortunately boils at a lower temperature than water, and as the spirit is driven off it ascends into the neck of the still, passes along the lyne arm and is then cooled by running water either in a tank enclosing the spiral worm or in a condenser. This first separation is coarse and unpalatable and is known as low wines.

To achieve a potable spirit there has to be a second distillation and there are two distilleries in Scotland where three distillations are considered desirable. The stillman, examining the spirit as it flows into the sample and spirit safe after its much slower second distillation, uses both thermometers and hydrometers to decide the most propitious time for collecting the 'middle cut' of the run. The first and last part of the distillation – the foreshots and feints – are diverted to await further distillation.

The safe, a brass-bound glass box, is kept under excise locks. When the whisky, at this stage as clear and as colourless as the spring water from which it is made, is collected in a special receiver, the quantity produced from each mash is checked by the excise officer.

From the receiver, the whisky is 'filled' into oak casks either at the distillery or at a bonded warehouse where it will have been taken by tanker. Once in wood, the whisky is forced by law to remain maturing for a minimum of three years; most whiskies are kept for five years and the finest are matured for much longer periods. It is estimated that throughout Scotland every year about 13 million proof gallons (59,098 million litres) of whisky are oxidised and evaporate into thin air during the maturation process.

After maturing, the malt whisky is either sold as a single malt or mixed with other malts to make what is known as a 'vatted' malt. A growing amount of malt whisky is exported in bulk. Japan is the biggest customer. In 1978, of the 80·6 million proof gallons of malt whisky distilled in Scotland, $10\frac{1}{2}$ million gallons were exported and of that $6\frac{1}{2}$ million gallons went to Japan. The rest went to Spain, Argentina, Brazil and South Africa, where when blended with locally produced spirit it competes on advantageous terms with imported Scotch.

Eighty-five per cent of all the malt whisky produced is eventually blended with grain whisky (in an average proportion of 30 per cent malt to 70 per cent grain) to produce the two thousand and more blended and branded whiskies. About 96 million gallons of grain whisky are produced annually using maize with a small addition of malted and unmalted barley. Scotland's twelve large grain distilleries are located mainly in the Central Lowlands, and the manufacture of grain whisky is carried out on an unromantic and industrial scale. The maize is cooked under pressure, a shock treatment which bursts the starch cells and allows the enzymes in the accompanying malt to convert this starch into saccharines. Wash is produced in a continuous flow and pumped into the top of a high column called a rectifier. From here it goes to a second column, known as an analyser, where rising steam strips off the alcohol. The alcohol vapour re-enters the rectifier where, economically, the wash descending in its zig-zag pipes condenses the alcoholic steam. Grain whisky, like malt whisky, is matured in oak for a minimum of three years, but is generally regarded as greatly inferior to malt whisky.

A dram at *Glenfarclas*

Appendices

Distilleries which can be visited

Not all distilleries have the staff or the facilities to entertain parties of visitors. Some do and some of these are listed here. If you are in doubt, check with the local tourist office. Some distilleries which do accept small parties prefer advance notice: it is wise to ring beforehand. Few distilleries receive visitors outside the summer tourist season; if in doubt phone the manager's office and ask.

Auchroisk (1973–4) Mulben, Banffshire.
In the entrance hall you will see a Victorian steam engine once used for milling malt at *Strathmill* distillery in Keith.
Blair Athol (1825) Pitlochry, Perthshire.
The water used in the distillery comes from Ben Vrackie.
Glenburgie (1829) Forres, Morayshire.
Takes its name from nearby sixteenth-century Burgie castle, of which all that remains today is a six-storied tower. *Glenburgie* malt whisky is found in *Glencraig* vatted malt.
Glendronach (1826) Forgue by Huntley.
Owned by Teachers, the distillery is named after the Dronac burn whence its water comes.
Glenfarclas (1836) Ballindalloch, Banffshire.
The reception centre is panelled with wood from the S.S. *Australia* and there is a re-creation of a smuggler's bothy complete with illicit still. *Glenfarclas* malt whisky has received the gold medal of the Club Oenologique for eight years in succession.
Glenfiddich (1886–7) and *Balvenie* (1892) Dufftown, Banffshire.
The most successfully exported malt whisky in the world. An excellent visitor centre which is more widely visited than any other in Scotland.
Glengarioch (1798) Old Meldrum, Aberdeenshire.
Glen Grant (1840) Rothes, Morayshire.
Now part of the Seagram empire. The malt is bottled at a variety of ages and proofs and is considered to be one of the top five in the country.
The Glenlivet (1824) Glenlivet, Banffshire.
Has a delightful visitor centre with a representation of a whisky bothy. There is

no more distinguished whisky in the world.

Glenmoray-Glenlivet (1897) Elgin. Steam engine still to be seen; stands on the right bank of the river Lossie.

Glenugie (1873) Peterhead. Takes its water from the Ugie burn.

Macallan (1824) Craigellachie. No single malt is sold younger than ten years old; one of the greats.

Strathisla (1786) Keith, Banffshire.

Near the oldest building in Keith, Milton Tower, this is reputed to be the oldest productive distillery in Scotland, a claim which might be disputed by *Bowmore* on Islay which celebrated its bicentenary in 1979.

Strathmill (1891) Keith, Banffshire.

Began life, like several other nineteenth-century distilleries, as a flour mill. Noted in contemporary times as the first distillery to send its whisky south for blending by tanker – the vehicle was christened 'Whisky Galore'.

Tamdhu (1896) Strathspey, Banffshire.

The site for this distillery was dictated by the proximity of the Strathspey Railway. Closed in the sixties, the little wooden station has been transformed into a visitor centre.

Visitors leaving *Glenfarclas*.

Tormore (1960) Advie, Morayshire.

The first Highland distillery to be built in the twentieth century.

A whisky trail has been devised by the Department of Leisure, Recreation and Tourism of the Grampian Regional Council, and copies can be obtained from local tourist offices. Disappointingly, it only takes in four distilleries (*Glenfiddich, Glenfarclas, Tamdhu* and *Strathisla*) on its 62-mile scenic route. Sixty of Scotland's 117 malt distilleries lie in the Grampian region. There are of course, equally well-known distilleries in the Lowlands and in other parts of the Highlands and Islands. The following forty working distilleries were all established 150 years ago or more, many of them rooted in the context of illicit distilling.

In the Lowlands: *Auchentoshan* (Dalmuir), *Bladnoch* (Wigtown), *Littlemill* (Bowling), *Rosebank* (Falkirk), *Springbank* (Campbeltown).

On the Islands: *Talisker* (Skye), *Highland Park* (Orkney), *Ardbeg, Bowmore, Lagavulin, Laphroaig, Port Ellen* (Islay), *Jura* (Jura), *Ledaig* (temporarily closed, Mull).

In the Highlands: *Aberlour, Balbair* (Edderton), *Balmenach* (Cromdale), *Banff, Ben Nevis* (Fort William), *Blair Athol* (Pitlochry), *Brechin, Cardow* (Knockando), *Clynelish* (Brora), *Edradour* (Pitlochry), *Fettercairn, Glenburgie* (Forres), *Glencadam* (Brechin), *Glendronach* (Huntly), *Glengarioch* (Old Meldrum), *The Glenlivet, Glenturret* (Crieff), *Lochnagar* (Balmoral), *Macallan* (Craigellachie), *Millburn* (Inverness), *Miltonduff* (Elgin), *Mortlach* (Dufftown), *Oban, Pulteney* (Wick), *Royal Brackla* (Nairn), *Strathisla* (Keith), *Teaninich* (Alness).

Glossary

Anker A cask holding just over 8 imperial gallons.

Bere A hardy, early-ripening variety of barley once grown extensively in the Highlands and Islands.

Bothy A one-roomed hut often built with stone and roofed with turf.

Butt A large oak cask holding 110 gallons.

Congenerics The impurities and trace elements (aldehydes and esters) which give malt whisky its characteristic taste and flavour.

Dog A device designed to extract whisky illicitly from the cask.

Draff The spent grain left in the mash tun after the liquor has been drained off.

Gauger The local name for excisemen, one of whose functions was to gauge malt so that the duty payable could be assessed.

Green Malt Undried malted barley.

Grieve A farm overseer.

Hogshead An oak cask containing 55–56 gallons.

Kiln The pagoda-roofed building in which green malt was spread on perforated iron floors to be heat-dried and peated.

Malt Barley which has been steeped in water, allowed to sprout and dried in a kiln.

Mashing The infusion of cereal with hot water.

Mash Tun The huge vessel in which the mashing process occurs.

Mountain A strong, rich, dark wine made from grapes grown in the Malaga region of Spain. The best Mountain was grown on mountain slopes around Archidona, Antequera and Velez-Malaga.

Orramen (Orra men) Farm-workers employed to do odd jobs.

Pot Still A large, onion-shaped copper vessel. In the wash still the fermented wash is heated until all the alcohol is driven off; in the spirit still the final potable spirit is produced.

Worm A coiled copper tube, cooled by running water, through whose diminishing length the alcoholic vapours condense.

Worts The liquid, containing the sugars of the malt, which is drawn off after the malt has been mashed with warm water.

Books worth reading

Alexander, William *Sketches of Northern Rural Life* (1877)

Andrews, Allen *The Whisky Barons* (Jupiter Books, 1977)

Barnard, Alfred *The Whisky Distilleries of the United Kingdom* (Harper, 1887)

Boswell, James *Journal of a Tour to the Hebrides* (1785)

Brander, Michael *A Guide to Scotch Whisky* (Johnston & Bacon, 1975)

Bruce Lockhart, Sir Robert *Scotch* (Putnam, 1951)

Cameron, David Kerr *The Ballad and the Plough* (Gollancz, 1978)

Cooper, Derek *Guide to the Whiskies of Scotland* (Pitman, 1978)

Daiches, David *Scotch Whisky* (André Deutsch, 1969)

Fraser, Duncan *Glen of the Rowan Trees* (Standard Press, 1978)

Gillespie, Malcolm *Memorial and Case of Malcolm Gillespie* (1826)

Gunn, Neil M. *Whisky and Scotland* (Routledge, 1933)

Grant, Elizabeth of Rothiemurchus *Memoirs of a Highland Lady 1797–1827* (John Murray, 1950)

Grant, I. F. *Highland Folk Ways* (Routledge, 1961)

Haldane, A. R. B. *The Drove Roads of Scotland* (Nelson, 1952)

Hart-Davis, Duff *Monarchs of the Glen* (Jonathan Cape, 1978)

Henderson, John A. *Annals of Lower Deeside* (1892)

Hume, John *The Industrial Archaeology of Scotland. The Highlands and Islands* (Batsford, 1977)

Macculloch, John *The Highlands and Western Isles of Scotland* (1824)

Macdonald, Aeneas *Whisky* (The Porpose Press, 1930)

Macdonald, Ian *Smuggling in the Highlands* (Eneas Mackay, 1914)

McEwan, John *Who Owns Scotland?* (EUSPB, 1979)

Mackenzie, Osgood *A Hundred Years in the Highlands* (Arnold, 1922)

Millman, R. N. *The Making of the Scottish Landscape* (Batsford, 1975)

Mitchell, Joseph *Reminiscences of my Life in the Highlands* (1883–4)

Moss, Michael S., John R. Hume *The Making of Scotch Whisky* (James & James, 1981)

Murphy, Brian *The World Book of Whisky* (Collins, 1978)

Pattullo, Dione and Derek Cooper *Enjoying Scotch* (Johnston & Bacon, 1980)

Pennant, Thomas *Tour in Scotland* (1771)

Richards, Eric *The Leviathan of Wealth* (Routledge, 1973)

Rogers, Rev. Charles *Social Life in Scotland* (1884)

Ross, James *Whisky* (Routledge, 1970)

St John, Charles *The Wild Sports of the Highlands* (1846)

Shand, A. J. *Letters from the Highlands* (1883)

Sillett, S. W. *Illicit Scotch* (Impulse Books, 1970)

Simpson, E. D. *Scottish Castles* (H.M.S.O., 1959)

Simpson, W. D. *The Book of Glenbuchat* (1942)

Somers, Robert *Letters from the Highlands* (1848; Melvens Bookshop, Inverness, 1977)

Stewart, David *Sketches of the Character, Manners and Present State of the Highlanders of Scotland* (1825)

Victoria, Queen *Leaves from the Journal of Our Life in the Highlands 1848–61*

Whittle, Tyler *Victoria and Albert at Home* (Routledge, 1980)

Wilson, Ross *Scotch, its History and Romance* (David & Charles, 1973)

Jock's Road From Tomintoul there were almost certainly many routes scaling the formidable eastern slopes of the Cairngorms but they are no longer clearly visible. Our route takes us along General Wade's road over the notorious Lecht, the A939 to Braemar. Train after trai of whisky passed through Braemar along Jock's Road which starts just south of Braemar at Auchallater (155883).

The start of the walk is clearly signposted from the road and the estate road as far as Loch Callater is easy going. After that the path is poor and its a case of picking your way through bog along the river or leaving the swampy path and following the line of the river at a slightly higher level along the hillside. It takes between six and eight hours to get from Auchallater to Glen Doll lodge. On the Tolmount pass the path becomes more distinct once you have quitted the Invercauld estate. There are magnificent and rewarding views from the flat plateau of the Tolmount (3,143 ft). The descent to Glen Doll lodge is fairly rugged. From there the motor road carries on down to Glen Clova celebrated for its alpine flora, along the little B955 road to Kirriemuir and on to Dundee through Glamis.

The Cabrach This famous upland plateau ı bleak moors and deer forests ringed by magnificent mountain peaks is now crossed by an excellent road. From Dufftown to Donside along the A941,then take the B9002 to pass the Motte of Auchindoir, an earth and timber fortress on which was built in the thirteenth century a superb church now in ruins. Then join the A97 to pass Kildrummy Castle and Gardens and Glen Buchat castle. From there you join up with the Ladder route to Glen Tanar. (Approximate time 1½hours).

The Fungle The Fungle path from Aboyne to Tarfside starts just west of the south end of the bridge over the Dee near Birsemore (523968). The first part which is clearly marked rises steeply up a wooded glen crossing a stream after about half a mile and then past the Rest and Be Thankful viewpoint. The best way then is to follow the burn south for a further two or three miles and pick up the Birse Castle Estate road which eventually leads to the west of the Castle which is privately owned. From the Water of Feugh south of Birse Castle the Fungle track is easy to follow as it winds south for seven or eight miles where it joins another estate road and continues a further couple of miles down to the small village of Tarfside, in its heyday a metropolis of illicit distilling. From Tarfside, crossing the North Esk, the old Whisky Road goes where it is also known as the Priest's Road. It then iontinues down through the Clash of Wirren to Glenlethnot. Here at Tullybardine you'll see a sign indicating the Whisky Road. The path can be traversed either on foot or by a minor metalled road passing between the two ancient hill forts of the Brown and White Cathertons (or Caterthun). Another way to join the Fungle is to take the pleasant motor road the B976 from Strachan to Birse Castle and walk from there.

The Whisky Road or Priest's Road runs from Upper Glenesk at Tarfside by way of the Clash of Wirren (2000ft) then down to Tullybardine and Glen Lethnot. It is known as the Priest's Road because at one time the Minister at Lochlee (Glenesk) also took the services at Lethnot and had to cross this mountain track to preach to the other half of his flock.

(Approximately three hours from Tarfside to the Cathertons).

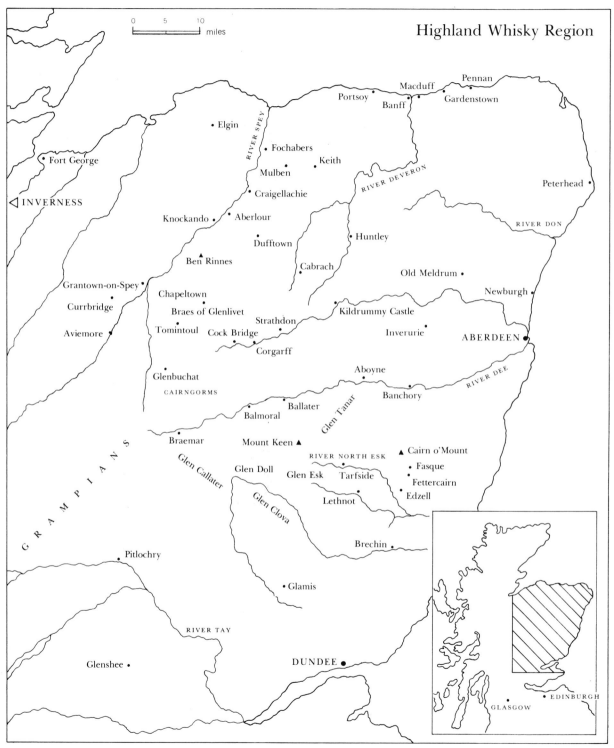

Highland Whisky Region

0 5 10 miles

Fort George

◁ INVERNESS

Elgin

RIVER SPEY

Portsoy
Banff
Macduff
Pennan
Gardenstown

Fochabers

Keith

Mulben

RIVER DEVERON

Peterhead

Craigellachie

Knockando
Aberlour

Huntley

RIVER DON

Dufftown

Cabrach

Old Meldrum

Newburgh

Ben Rinnes ▲

Grantown-on-Spey

Chapeltown

Kildrummy Castle

Currbridge

Braes of Glenlivet

Strathdon

Inverurie

ABERDEEN

Aviemore

Tomintoul

Cock Bridge

Corgarff

Glenbuchat

CAIRNGORMS

Aboyne

Glen Tanar

Banchory

RIVER DEE

Ballater

Balmoral

Braemar

Mount Keen ▲

Cairn o'Mount ▲

RIVER NORTH ESK

Fasque

Glen Callater

Glen Doll

Glen Esk

Tarfside

Fettercairn

G R A M P I A N S

Glen Clova

Lethnot

Edzell

Brechin

Pitlochry

Glamis

RIVER TAY

Glenshee

DUNDEE ●

GLASGOW

EDINBURGH

Recommended Ordnance Survey Northern and Central Scotland sheets 2 and 4, 1:250,000

The Ladder The Ladder Hills command superb views as far as the peaks of Perthshire. The Ladder path starts from Chapeltown at Braes of Glenlivet. Turn east on the minor lane passing East Auchavaich (250206) and you then pass Ladderfoot and walk up the steep Ladder burn and find a magnificent view at the top. Five miles on you pass Duffdefiance and then on to Strathdon past an impressive motte and Strathdon bridge. From there you'll find motor roads to Dinnet crossing the Dee to Glen Tanar. Here the road is known as the Mounth though its part of the Ladder route. (An alternative whisky route from Braes of Glenlivet is from Suie (277248) to Glen Buchat lodge and along the motor road to Glen Buchat castle to rejoin the Ladder).

The route through Glen Tanar estate is enviably well signposted and passes the Braeloine Visitor Centre. The road climbs over the western shoulder of Mount Keen, down a zig-zag route also known as the Ladder and past the Queen's Well to Glen Mark. From here are a number of routes over Rowan Hill to Tarfside leading to the Whisky Road or Priest's Road.

(Time: Chapeltown or Suie to Donside, approximately four hurs. Glen Tanar to Tarfside about six to eight hours.)

Cairn o Mount The road linking Banchory and Fettercairn on the B974 over a summit of 1,475 feet is rich in historical associations. Take the road from Banchory-Strachan through natural pine forests down to the Bridge of Dye then over the high pass and down a very steep road to Clatterin' Brig. From here the whisky-runners took a back road behind Fasque and there were many confrontations with the revenue men. 'Donald's Bed' is a hallowed site where one of the whisky men was alain and his body lay in a ferny hollow for twenty years before being found by foresters.

The B974 continues from Clatterin' Brig to Fettercairn and Edzell and on to the cathedral town of Brechin. From Brechin the routes are south to Glamis, passing the remarkable Aberlemno Stones.

Chapeltown to Well of the Lecht The old whisky road from Chapeltown of Glenlivet (24520) past Scalan and on over Carn Dulach down to the Well of the Lecht passing an old mill near General Wade's road. No doubt the military road was used by smugglers – today it's an exhilarating and easy one hour drive over the Lecht to Tomintoul and down to Donside.

The Beatshach The Beatshach is an old whisky route off the A95 west of Aberlour to Edinvillie. Its a wild and solitary route but easily driveable and takes in several distilleries including *Glenlivet* itself, *Braes of Glenlivet* and *Allt a Bhainne*.

These are just a few of the walks which follow or cross the old smuggling tracks. Hill-walking if you have the right clothes and good stout boots and the relevant Ordnance Survey maps (1:50,000 is recommended) is a constant delight. It is worth remembering that the climate on the higher hills is sub-Arctic and the average temperature at 3000 feet is 10 degree lower than at sea level. Even in June winter conditions may be encountered over 3000 feet. Ill-equipped hill-walkers, however, are a danger to themselves, and have repeatedly involved the rescue services in these areas in expensive and hazardous missions. Inexperienced walkers may find themselves subjected to rigours which they have previously associated with the depths of winter. High wind velocity is almost as important as a low temperature in causing hypothermia, and is often associated also with conditions which change rapidly from near ideal o potentially disastrous. Never, therefore, set out for a day's walking without wind and weather-proof clothing: and always follow the example of the serious climber in leaving word of your itinerary and expected time of return.

The Department of Leisure, Recreation & Tourism of the Grampian Region has produced an excellent publication called *Hill-walking in the Grampian Region* (45p) which is worth every penny.

Index

Place names in italic indicate distilleries
Page numbers in italic indicate photographs

DIAGNOSTIC IMAGING
CHEST

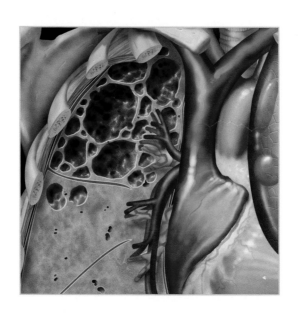